Bold & Beautiful
PAPER FLOWERS

More Than **50** Easy Paper Blooms and
Gorgeous Arrangements You Can Make at Home

Chantal Larocque

PAGE STREET
PUBLISHING CO.

PAGE STREET
PUBLISHING CO.

First published in 2017 by

Page Street Publishing Co.

27 Congress Street, Suite 105

Salem, MA 01970

www.pagestreetpublishing.com

Distributed by Macmillan, sales in Canada by The Canadian Manda Group.

21 20 19 18 17   1 2 3 4 5

ISBN-13: 978-1-62414-447-9

ISBN-10: 1-62414-447-0

Library of Congress Control Number: 2017938093

Cover and book design by Page Street Publishing Co.

Cover photo and photos on pages 152 and 170 by Caro Photo

Photography by Chantal Larocque

Author headshot on page 188 by Karen Casey Photography

Printed and bound in China

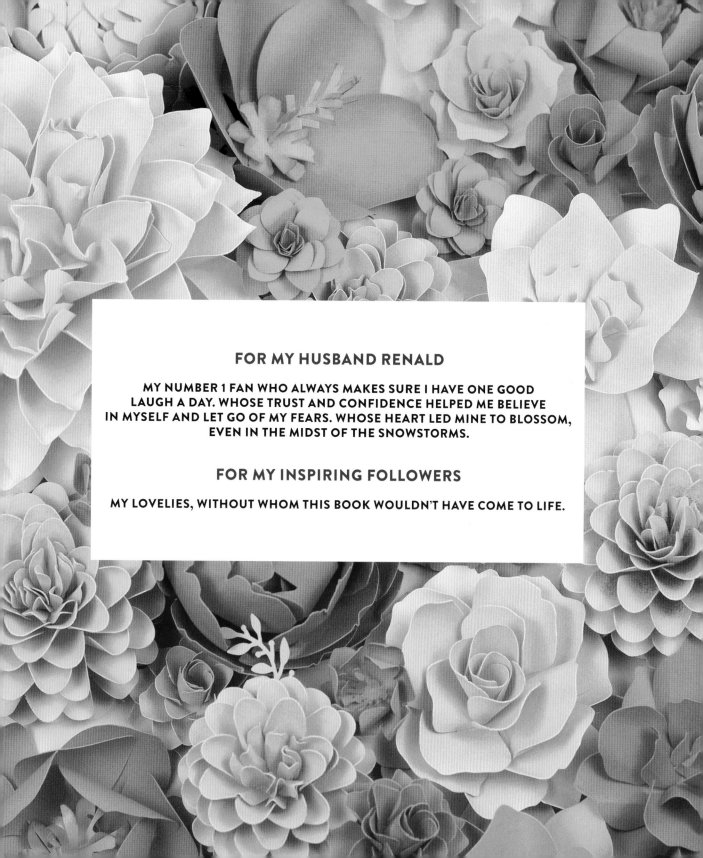

FOR MY HUSBAND RENALD

MY NUMBER 1 FAN WHO ALWAYS MAKES SURE I HAVE ONE GOOD
LAUGH A DAY. WHOSE TRUST AND CONFIDENCE HELPED ME BELIEVE
IN MYSELF AND LET GO OF MY FEARS. WHOSE HEART LED MINE TO BLOSSOM,
EVEN IN THE MIDST OF THE SNOWSTORMS.

FOR MY INSPIRING FOLLOWERS

MY LOVELIES, WITHOUT WHOM THIS BOOK WOULDN'T HAVE COME TO LIFE.

CONTENTS

CHAPTER ONE

THE PAPER GARDEN IN FULL BLOOM!   **13**

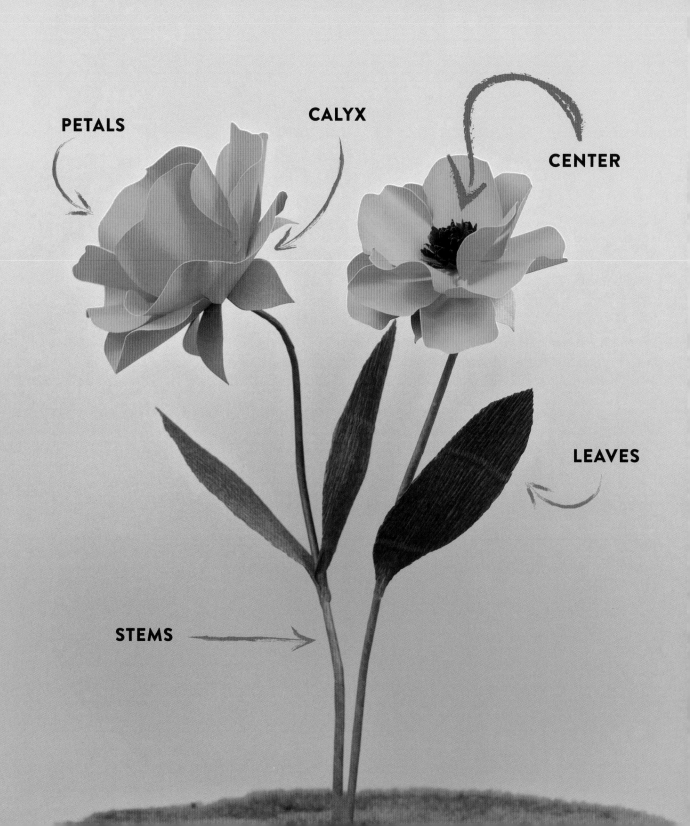

PETALS

CALYX

CENTER

LEAVES

STEMS

Forever in Bloom: Why You'll Love Paper Flowers

Flowers are universally loved. They have a knack for effortlessly making just about any room more beautiful and any person in their presence a little happier. That being said, I'd venture to say that even the prettiest natural blooms fall short sometimes. Once cut and arranged, they can be enjoyed for only a short while. Paper flowers, on the other hand, last forever. Add the facts that they are fragrance-free, don't require any upkeep or water and are made from renewable resources, and choosing paper flowers over real ones soon becomes a no-brainer.

When I first discovered the world of paper flower crafts, I was immediately excited and quickly consumed with all the possibilities. From intricate petals to oversized blooms—there were no limits to what I could create. Sometimes, my head literally felt like it would burst with all these ideas! Not to mention that I hadn't even gotten around to realizing that designing made-up flowers from my imagination could open up a whole other realm of options for my clients! I guess you can say I fell hard for this new-to-me art form, and a lasting passion for it was born.

Over the years, I've lost count of how many petals I've cut, curled and glued. But you know what? To this day, I get excited when a flower is taking shape in front of my eyes, and I want you to feel that same exhilaration. That's why I'm so thrilled to finally be able to share my excitement and passion for paper flower artistry with you through this book.

Tips and tricks aside, I want you to know that getting started in this craft does not require fancy tools or a big investment. The basics—a pair of scissors, a glue gun and the tip of an old paintbrush—will take you very far. This art form is all about having fun while experimenting with different shapes and colors and improvising with what other tools you have available. You'll soon realize that your own surroundings offer endless inspiration and that there is no set way of making flowers of all sizes out of paper. After all, as with any handmade item, personality will give your blooms that extra-special something.

My hope for you is not only to learn skills through this collection of projects, but also that it brings you a little something more: happy vibes when you transform pieces of paper into impressive works of art for yourself or loved ones. So much of my own satisfaction for creating comes from knowing that I am providing clients and friends with unique and lasting florals that complement their celebrations and honor their vision. As you'll soon realize when you get started, flowers make just about any heart smile . . . and that is the best gift of all.

xx

TOOLS AND MATERIALS

When I first started making paper flowers, I sought guidance from scrapbooking video tutorials. That's where I noticed how many of the fancy tools the pros used could easily be replaced by common household items. When possible, I like to use thrifty hacks to make my floral creations, and I encourage you to follow my lead. A simple sushi stick makes for a perfect curling tool, the mouse pad on your desk can double as a molding mat and the rounded end of a paint brush or pen can be use as your dimensional tool! I recommend using 65-pound cardstock for all of the flower projects in this book. I've found this is the best type of paper, and it is what I use to make my blooms for my business. However, feel free to experiment or improvise and amend the materials according to what is available to you. For many of the images you'll enjoy in this book, I've used vases, vessels and containers found in my home, at my local thrift store and borrowed from stylish friends.

PROJECT STEPS DEFINITIONS

In this book, you'll find that I regularly use the same steps to transform the petal templates into dimensional blooms. Getting comfortable with the following techniques will speed up your understanding of the projects a great deal.

CURL

Curling is done by using a narrow rounded tool like a chopstick or a knitting needle to curl the edge of a petal inward or outward.

MOLD/PRESS

Place the paper on a soft work surface such as a mouse pad or molding mat. Using your dimensional tool or the rounded tip of the end of a paint brush, press gently into the paper, making a circular motion. The soft foam working area will encourage the paper to change shape as you apply pressure, without creating an undesirable fold or crease.

SHAVE

Have you ever curled gift-wrapping ribbon using the edge of a scissor blade? This technique uses the same principle, except I like to use wooden sticks of different sizes to execute the motion because they create a smoother curve and won't scratch the paper.

PIERCE

This is the action required when mounting a wire to a calyx or petal layer. I like to use a corsage pin to first pierce a little hole in the middle of the template. It makes it much easier to skewer the wire through the paper!

BASIC TECHNIQUES

TEMPLATES

The templates provided at the back of this book are exactly the right size you'll need to create the flowers and leaves shown in the photos (with the exception of the large-scale blooms in Chapter 7). Once you are comfortable with the techniques, you can certainly use a copier to enlarge or diminish their sizes to create a different look. What I personally do is trace all my templates onto cardboard with their specific numbers. This way, they are sturdier to use, which makes tracing onto cardstock for each project easy.

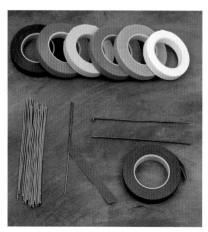

USING FLORAL TAPE

Most projects in this book involve wire stems. I buy cloth- or paper-covered stems so I don't have to cover the stems with tape, but this technique is good to know if covered stems are not available—tape-covered stems look so much nicer than just bare wire! You'll also need to understand this wire-wrapping technique right off the bat, since it's also quite useful when adding leaves to stems or joining multiple blooms together.

To learn this very specific skill I went straight to the source: an awesome local florist. She kindly took the time to demonstrate exactly how it's done and gently reminded me that only practice makes perfect. So, back I went to my dining room table to do just that! Many finger cramps and a few hours later, I was finally holding twelve beautifully wrapped stems.

The number one trick to remember with floral tape is that the glue is activated only once the tape is stretched. Always start taping at the top of the stem, holding the wire firmly with one hand. Gently stretch the tape around the wire on an angle, wrapping toward the bottom of the stem while keeping the tape taut. For a smooth finish, take care to only overlap the edge of the tape slightly and pinch the tape to the wire with your fingers as you go. I can't stress the stretching part enough, since it makes the tape stick to itself. When taping two wires together, ensure the wires are straight, not twisted together, to create a more polished look.

While you are practicing the wire-wrapping technique, why not prepare a whole bunch? This way, whenever you need to mount a bloom to a wire, you'll have a little stack of wrapped stems all ready to go!

MOUNTING A BLOOM ON A WIRE

Mounting a bloom to a wire stem in a sturdy way is one of the most essential steps to bringing your paper flowers to life. Choosing the right wire for this technique is very important. There are different gauges that I like to use, and my choice depends simply on the size of the bloom. The higher the gauge number, the thinner the wire will be. So, for most flowers, I use a 20-gauge wire, and for mini blooms and smaller leaves, I like to use a 26-gauge wire.

When I first began mounting my scrapbooking blooms on wires, I struggled to find a method I liked. But after a few attempts, I found the method that worked best for me, and to this day, I'm still using those same simple steps. The technique I'm sharing with you here works very well based on several years of client feedback. Trust me: With the right amount of hot glue, your bloom will remain firmly mounted on its wire!

Ready? First you'll need to have a few tape-covered wire stems, cut-out calyxes (templates on page 186), wire cutters, a corsage pin, pliers and a hot glue gun with glue on hand. Start by creating a coil at the end of your wire with the pliers, then bend the coil perpendicular to the wire. Next, pierce the center of the calyx with a corsage pin to create a small hole. You can now gently skewer the calyx and slide it up toward the coil until the coil is sitting directly on top of it. Add a bit of glue between the calyx and the coil. Once the glue is dry and the calyx is fixed to the coil, add a fair amount of hot glue over the middle part of the calyx to secure it to the flower. Hold the bloom in place for a few seconds or until you feel the flower has adhered to the wire and won't budge.

MAKING THE LEAVES

Leaves are not only pretty, they are also perfect for adding texture, depth and fullness to any arrangement. With practice, making leaves and even cutting original leaf shapes freehand will become second nature to you!

The following instructions apply to every style of leaf included in this book. You'll find my own templates on page 171. For an easy hack, I suggest scanning or photocopying my leaves templates and increasing or decreasing the size of the templates before printing them. This will help you trace the leaves at a different scale. The Fern Envy project (page 129) is a great example, since you can use the same fern template scaled at different sizes to make the arrangement look more interesting and realistic. I like to use both cardstock and crepe paper to make leaves. Both materials require the same technique described below.

To add a leaf to a wire, dab a bit of glue on the narrow part of the leaf and squeeze it with your fingers around the wire. Apply the floral tape at the base of the leaf and gently stretch tape around the wire on an angle, wrapping toward the bottom of the stem while keeping the tape taut. Every time you add a leaf, you should wrap the wire with tape all the way to the bottom so the leaf looks like it was there all along.

The Paper Garden in Full Bloom!

That's right! The next few pages will teach you easy step-by-step methods for creating fabulous paper flower blooms.

You'll notice that I often use the same petal templates as a starting point for the design of completely different flowers. For example, the Rose (page 15) and the Sophia (page 39) blooms start with the same larger petal template, which is then modified to create a completely different look.

Follow along and you'll become comfortable customizing my templates to create your very own unique flower designs in no time!

Let's get started and transform your crafting space (or your dining room table) into a Paper Garden in Full Bloom, one flower at a time.

THE ROSE

"I've come to believe that the true splendor of roses shines through their reflection in the eyes of our loved ones. That is why we give roses to people we love; to show them the reflection of beauty and splendor of love in our own eyes, as we see it in their eyes." —*Mawuena Addo*

With beautiful words like these, there is not much else I can add, other than to say that the rose has always been a timeless symbol of love, beauty and balance.

. . . . .

Template P-01 x 4 (page 171)
Template P-02 x 2 (page 171)
Curling tool
Molding mat
Dimensional tool
Hot glue gun and glue sticks
Template C-01 (optional, page 186)

1 - Once your six pieces are cut, using your curling tool, curl each petal inward. Repeat this step with each of the six petal layers.

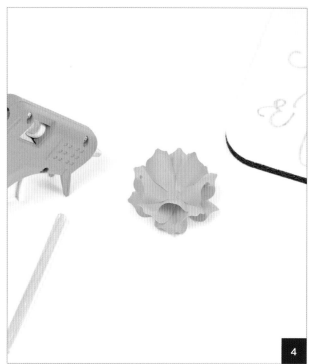

2 - Using the molding mat as a working surface, gently press the center of three of the four P-01 petal layers with the dimensional tool—make sure the curled petals are facing down.

3 - Now press the remaining P-01 petal layer with the curls facing up this time. Repeat that step with the two smaller (P-02) petal layers. Then close the petals inward with your fingers to create a bud shape.

4 - Time to assemble! Starting with the larger petal layers with curls facing down, dab a small amount of glue in the center of the petals, staggering the placement of each layer to create a full bloom.

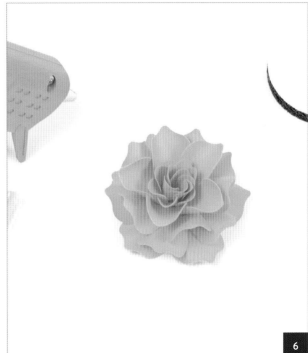

5 - Then secure the remaining large petal layer with the curls facing up.

6 - Do the same as step 5 with the two bud shapes, one inside the other.

7 - To finish, gently curl the last of the largest petal layer (P-01) outward and voilà! You've made a beautiful little rose!

Repeat all these easy steps to make as many roses as your heart desires!

Follow the basic steps found on page 11 to mount the Rose on wire stems using template C-01 for the calyx.

THE ROYAL ROSE

"I'd rather have roses on my table than diamonds on my neck." —Emma Goldman

No other flower is as recognizable as the rose. No other flower conveys love and passion like the rose, either. For the longest time roses have enjoyed the honor of being the most popular flowers in the world. The reason for their popularity may be the wide variety of their color, size, fragrance and other attributes. The rose is one of a few styles I've designed through the years. Because they are so classy, you can add roses to most floral compositions for instant wow factor. I named this flower the Royal Rose because for me, its majestic design is an ode to this eternal classic belle.

. . . . .

Template P-05 x 3 (page 171)
Template P-06 x 2 (page 171)
Template P-07 x 1 (page 171)
Curling tool
Molding mat
Dimensional tool
Hot glue gun and glue sticks
Template C-01 x 1 (optional, page 186)

1 - Once all your petals are cut, curl the three P-05 petals with your curling tool, making sure to curl one side of each individual petal facing up and the other side facing down.

2 - Gently press the middle of the P-05 petals on the molding mat using your dimensional tool.

3 - Then, repeat the same curling steps as above for one of the P-06 petals.

4 - For the second P-06 petal as well as the P-07 petal, curl all sides of the individual petals facing up. Then, fold the petals tightly inward with your fingers to create two separate bud shapes.

5 - Using the glue gun, dab a small amount of glue in the center of the three P-05 petals and one of the P-06 petals. Stack these petals, making sure to stagger the placement of each layer to create a nice full bloom.

6 - Now you are ready to finish off the center of the flower. Start by inserting the smaller bud into the bigger one and securing them with a dab of glue. Finally, glue the newly created "double bud" into the center of the other previously stacked petals.

To mount the bloom on wire stems, follow the instructions found on page 11 of Basic Techniques, using template C-01 as the calyx.

THE PEONY

In my mind, no other flower can compete with the perfection of the Peony.

The silky petals, delicate shape, romantic shades and graceful foliage make this flower my all-time favorite, and I'm not alone. Brides plan their wedding dates around peony season. Flower enthusiasts plant them all through their gardens. Florists go crazy over all the different shades available from white to coral, yellow to red and every imaginable pink. Sadly, this bloom can only be enjoyed in nature for a very short time each year. That's the reason their paper counterparts have become such a hit! Over the years, I've perfected my paper peony design and this technique below is tried and true. I'm so excited to share it with you and just know you'll love including this fabulous flower in your home decor, bouquets and beyond!

· · · · ·

Template P-27 x 5 (page 173)
Template P-28 x 2 (page 174)
Circular measuring spoons
Molding mat
Dimensional tool
Hot glue gun and glue sticks
Curling tool
Crepe paper
Template L-03 x 2 (optional, page 182)
Template C-01 x 1 (optional, page 186)

1 - Once you've cut out all your petals, the first step is all about transforming them. Starting with the P-27 petals, use the tablespoon size of your measuring spoon set and gently press each individual petal into the rounded shape of the spoon with your thumb. Repeat this technique with each of these five P-27 pieces.

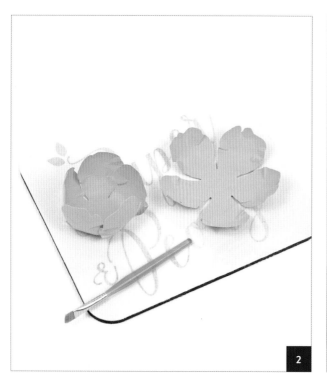

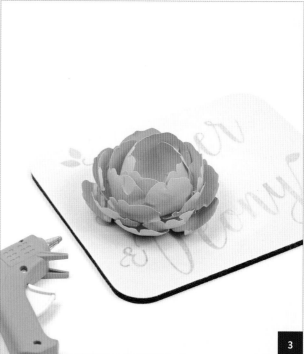

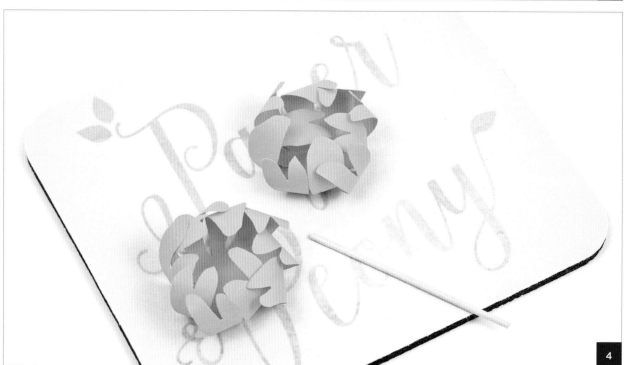

2 - When that's done, use the molding mat as your work surface and apply pressure to the middle of each petal layer with your dimensional tool. This motion should make your petals curl up.

3 - Once all five petals are shaped, dab a bit of hot glue at the heart of each petal and start stacking the layers, staggering them to create a full bloom.

4 - It's time to prepare the P-28 petals that will form the heart of the bloom. Using the edge of your scissor blade or your curling tool, "shave" all the individual petals from the middle of the petal toward the edge. This motion will make the petals curl inward.

5 - Now dab a bit of glue in the middle of one of these petals and nest the other inside it. Don't be afraid to use your fingers to arrange the petals and make them look loose and natural.

6 - Finally, add this double petal to the center of the stack created in step 5, using a bit more glue to secure it.

To mount this fabulous Peony on a wire stem and add the L-03 leaves, please refer to Basic Techniques on page 11. You will need the calyx template (C-01).

THE GARDENIA

The gardenia is a beautiful flower that looks perfect in all sorts of arrangements! This flower has some deep floral meanings; it actually says, "You are lovely," and it is even a symbol of a secret love. Ha! How about that! I like to use this fabulous bloom to embellish gifts and add wow-factor to bouquets, but I especially enjoy styling it in a three-bloom cluster that packs a pretty punch in any short vase. To create this small arrangement, you will need to make three gardenia blooms following and repeating the steps below three times. Once each gardenia is mounted on a stem, simply cut the stems to the desired length to complement your own vase.

. . . . .

Template P-01 x 1 (page 171)
Template P-02 x 1 (page 171)
Template P-04 x 3 (page 171)
Blending tool or sponge
Ink pad (in the color of your choosing)
Curling tool
Molding mat
Dimensional tool
Hot glue gun and glue sticks
Template L-01 x 1 (page 187)

1 - Once your petals are cut out, use the blending tool to lightly dab ink in a round shape at the center of each P-01 and P-02 petal layer—let dry for a few seconds before repeating on the other side of the template.

1

2 - Now, curl the edges of all three P-04 petal layers, using the skinny part of your curling tool. You'll want to make sure that all five petals on these templates are curled with one side facing up and the other side of the petal facing down.

3 - Using the same curling technique, curl all the edges of the P-01 and P-02 petal layers—both edges curled on the same side. Using the molding mat as your working surface, with the rounded tip of your dimensional tool, gently press the centers of the templates with the curls facing down.

4 - With the petal layers all prepped, you are now ready to use the glue gun. Starting with the larger petals (P-04), dab a small amount of glue in the center of the petal layers, staggering the petal placement of each layer to create a nice full bloom.

5 - Now glue the P-01 template (curls still facing down) onto the middle of the larger petals.

6 - Repeat Step 5 with the P-02 template.

7 - Time to add the finishing green touch. Pinch the tip of each of the five L-01 template leaves and curl all of them downward using the curling tool. Then dab on a bit of glue and adhere it to the bottom of the bloom.

To use as a gift bow, simply add a glue dot or double-sided tape and the bloom is ready to embellish your gift! Or if you wish to mount the blooms on wire stems, follow the instructions found on page 11 of Basic Techniques and use L-01 for the calyx. Don't forget, you will need to repeat all the steps three times to make a trio of three fabulous Gardenias!

THE DAHLIA

This majestic beauty looks just as fabulous alone in a tall vase as she does in an extravagant floral arrangement. Dahlias come in many varieties, but this paper version is inspired by the Hart's Tickle Pink. Can you believe this giant stunner can grow up to 5 feet (1.5 m) tall with a bloom measuring over 10 inches (25 cm) in diameter?

· · · · ·

Template P-10 x 6 (page 172)
Template P-11 x 2 (page 175)
Template P-12 x 2 (page 172)
Curling tool
Needle-nose pliers
Dimensional tool
Molding mat
Hot glue gun and glue sticks
Template C-01 x 1 (optional, page 186)

1 - Once all your petals are cut out, start by curling the edges of all ten petal layers inward using the curling tool.

2 - Then, using the pliers, gently pinch and twist the tips of each individual petal.

3 - Using the dimensional tool, gently press the center of all the petals except for two of the largest ones (P-10) and the two smaller petals (P-12) into the molding mat, with curls facing up. Then press the center of the remaining petals with the curls facing down.

4 - It's time to assemble the petals to create the bloom. Using one of the P-10 petals as a base, dab a small amount of glue in its center, making sure the curls of the petal are facing up. Add 4 of the larger petals one at a time, adding a bit of glue between each layer. Remember to stagger the petals as you add them to the stack to create a pretty, full bloom.

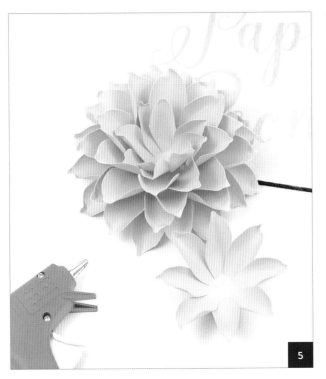

5 - Repeat the same steps with the two P-11 petal layers. You should now have only two P-12 petals and two P-10 petals remaining.

6 - Carefully dab a little hot glue on the inside of the two P-12 petals and nest them inside each other. The petals should be facing down to create a little bud. Once the bud is ready, add it to the center of the bloom.

7 - For the last step, turn the Dahlia upside down and add the other two P-10 petal layers to the base of the petal stack, with the curls facing the same direction as your stack. This will create a lovely petal skirt effect.

Refer to page 11 for the basic steps to mount the Dahlia on a wire stem, using template C-01 for the calyx.

THE FULL BLOOM DAHLIA

All dahlias are beautiful in their own way! I love them because they have the most perfect symmetry and come in a rainbow of color options, from warm coral to soft buttercream. It doesn't hurt that this flower is effortlessly cool too. Would you believe that each one has a unique name full of personality, like Café Au Lait, Mystique or Intrigue? How fun! The Full Bloom Dahlia we will be making in this project is inspired by the super-dense spherical variety, known for its smaller diameter.

. . . . .

Template P-14 x 8 (page 174)
Template P-15 x 1 (page 172)
Template P-16 x 1 (page 173)
Template P-17 x 2 (page 172)
Curling tool
Dimensional tool
Molding mat
Hot glue gun and glue sticks
Template C-01 x 1 (optional, page 186)

1 - Once all your petals are cut out, start by curling the edges of all twelve petals inward using the curling tool.

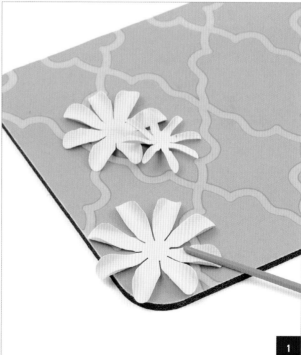

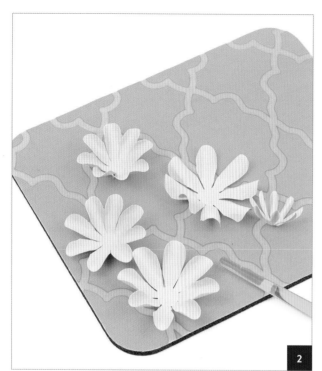

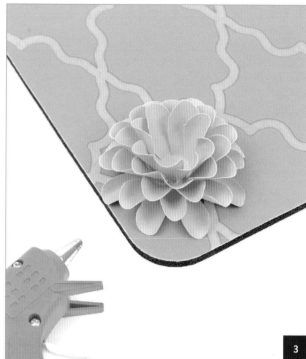

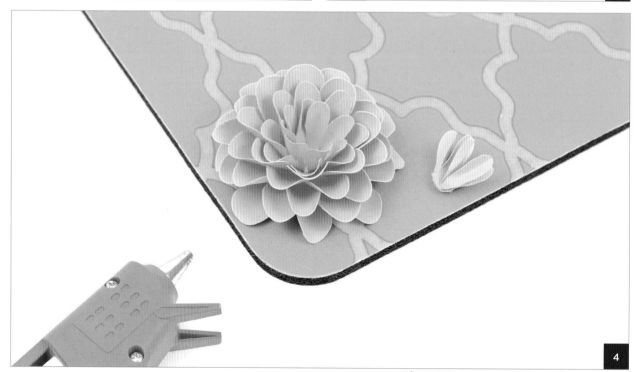

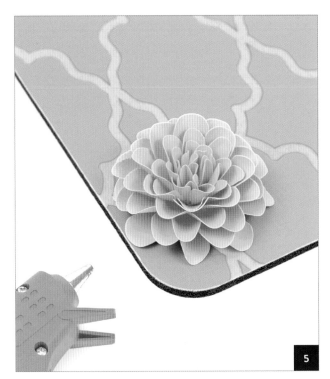

2 - Then, using the dimensional tool, gently press the center of all the petals, except for three of the largest ones (P-14) and the two smaller petals (P-17), with curls facing up, into the molding mat. For those remaining petals, press their centers into the molding mat with your dimensional tool, this time with the curls facing down.

3 - To assemble the Full Bloom Dahlia, use one of the P-14 petals as the base and dab a small amount of glue in its center, making sure the curls are facing up. Add one petal at a time, dabbing some glue between each layer. Don't forget to stagger the petals as you add them to the stack to create a dimensional effect!

4 - Repeat the same steps with petals P-15 and P-16. You should now have used all the petals except for the two smallest petals (P-17) and three of the largest ones (P-14). Carefully dab a little hot glue on the inside of the two P-17 petals and nest them inside each other. Keep the petals facing down and pinch them tightly with your fingers to create a little bud.

5 - Once the bud is ready, it's time to add it to the center of the bloom. Make sure you add a little glue there first, to secure it at the center of your flower.

6 - For the last step, turn the Full Bloom Dahlia upside down and add the other P-14 petals to the base of the petal stack with the curls facing the same direction as all the other ones. This will create a lovely petal skirt effect.

Refer to page 11 for the basic steps to mount the Full Bloom Dahlia on a wire stem and use template C-01 for the calyx.

THE SOPHIA

This is one quirky little bloom! It's inspired by the delightful azalea, one of Mother Nature's beautiful floral gifts. If this bloom could talk, it would say, "Think of all the beauty still left around you and be happy" (Anne Frank).

· · · · ·

Template P-01 x 4 (page 171)
Template P-18 x 1 (page 174)
Curling tool
Dimensional tool
Molding mat
Hot glue gun and glue sticks
Template C-01 x 1 (optional, page 186)

1 - Once your petals are cut out, use your curling tool to curl all the petals inward.

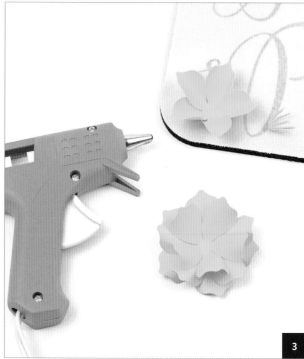

2 - Using your dimensional tool, gently press the center of three of the four P-01 petals into the molding mat, ensuring that the petals are facing downward. Then, use the same technique for the last large P-01 petal, this time with the curls of the petal facing up. Repeat this step one last time with petal P-18, which will be used as a stamen.

3 - To assemble the bloom, dab a small amount of glue in the center of one of the P-01 petals, with the curls facing down. Staggering the placement of each layer to create a full bloom, add two more large P-01 petals to the stack, making sure to add glue between each layer.

4 - Then, add the last P-01 petal on top, this time with the curls of the petal facing up.

5 - Add the last petal shape (P-18) to the center of the bloom, with a bit more glue.

6 - To finish, gently curl the top-most large petal outward so the stamen sticks out a bit.

To create a mini bouquet of five Sophia blooms, repeat all the steps five times! Follow the basic steps found on page 11 to mount these beauties on wire stems using template C-01 for the calyx.

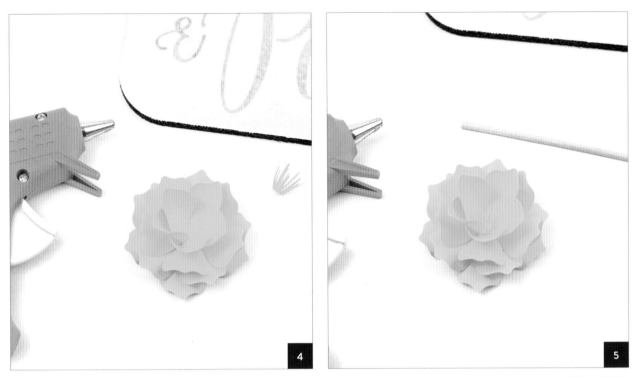

THE HIBISCUS

There are hundreds of species of hibiscus flowers, but they all need to live in hot, humid lands like India, Hawaii, Haiti or Malaysia. They come in a variety of sizes and colors, but most sport five-lobed petals around a stalked center. What better way to bring the tropics to your home than to make your own tropical flower bouquet!

· · · · ·

Template P-30 x 1 (page 174)
Template P-29 x 1 (page 175)
Template P-08 x 2 (page 171)
Template C-02 x 1 (page 186)
Wire stem
Hot glue gun and glue sticks
Ink pad and blending tool
Curling tool
Dimensional tool
Molding mat
Corsage pin

1 - First, cut out all the petals and the calyx. Then, wrap the long fringed stamen (P-30) around the wire stem in an angle going toward the bottom. Wrap it for about 2½ inches (5 cm). Don't forget to dab some glue as you wrap it around the stem to keep it in place.

2 - Then with your blending tool, rub a bit of ink on the top part only to add color.

3 - For the P-29 petal template, simply curl the petals in various directions to give the bloom a natural look.

4 - Then, use the dimensional tool and molding mat to press the middle part of the large petal layer.

5 - With your blending tool, rub a bit of ink on the edge of each P-08 petal.

6 - Squeeze each of the little petals tightly together.

7 - To assemble, dab a bit of glue on the P-08 petal layers and place them in the middle of the P-29 petal layer.

8 - Place the stacked petals on the molding mat and with a corsage pin, poke a hole in the middle.

9 - Insert the wire stem through the hole.

10 - To add visual interest, you can distress the edge of the calyx tips with dark ink. Skewer the calyx (C-02), dab some glue to it and fix it to the bottom of the bloom.

Repeat these steps to make as many tropical Hibiscus blooms as you'd like!

THE MARIGOLD

The cheerful golden-yellow marigold is synonymous with the sun. Sometimes referred to as the "herb of the sun," marigolds are thought to denote passion and creativity! This bloom is one of the first 3-D paper flowers I ever created. To this day, I love to include it in my floral compositions for a little dose of happiness! A simple trio of marigolds in a small vase is the perfect way to perk up any space.

. . . . .

Template P-20 x 4 (page 173)
Template P-21 x 2 (page 172)
Template P-22 x 2 (page 175)
Curling tool
Molding mat
Dimensional tool
Hot glue gun and glue sticks
Template C-01 x 1 (optional, page 186)

1 - Once your petals are cut out, use the skinny part of your curling tool to curl each individual petal inward on all templates except for the smallest petals (P-22).

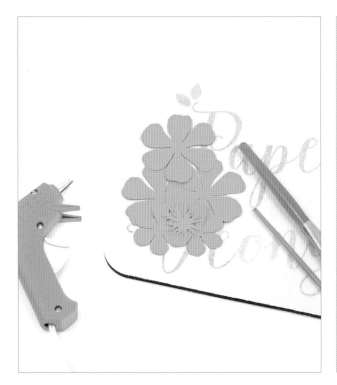

2 - Using the molding mat as a working surface, gently press the center of all the petal layers, including the tiny ones, with your dimensional tool. Make sure that the curled petals are facing up.

3 - To assemble the bloom, start by stacking the P-20 petals, dabbing a small amount of hot glue in the center of each piece as you go. Remember to stagger the placement of each layer as you add the petals to create a full bloom.

4 - Next, secure the two P-21 petals to the middle of the bloom with a bit more glue.

5 - Lastly, add the P-22 petals to the center, one inside the other, to make the heart of the Marigold look nice and full.

Repeat these easy steps three times to make a charming trio of Marigold flowers! Follow the basic steps found on page 11 to mount the Marigold on wire stems using template C-01 for the calyx.

Table 3

Emma Harte

Table 1

Darcy Miller

Table 5

Jamie Fraser

Table 6

Brianna Randall

Table 5

Claire Beauchamp

THE ROSETTA

Ahhh . . . the Rosetta! I first designed this little flower to jazz up escort cards for weddings and events. They became really popular because I could customize them to complement the venue and color palette of each occasion. Not to mention, they make a fantastic first impression and are a sweet keepsake for guests. The little Rosetta adorned with delicate leaves allows for enough room to write the names of your guests and their table number too.

. . . . .

Template P-21 x 6 (page 172)
Template L-04 x 2 (page 187)
Template C-02 x 1 (page 186)
Curling tool
Dimensional tool
Molding mat
Hot glue gun and glue sticks

1 - Once your petals, leaves and calyx are cut out, start by curling the edges of all six P-21 petals inward using the curling tool. Using the dimensional tool, gently press the center of all the petals into the molding mat, with curls facing up.

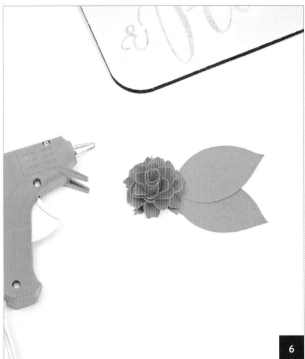

2 - Make a cone with two of the petals by squeezing them together. This way, you'll be able to nest them inside the middle of the bloom more easily.

3 - To assemble the Rosetta, use one of the larger petals as the base, with curls facing up. Dab a small amount of glue in its center and stack the other three petals on top, dabbing some glue between each layer. Don't forget to stagger the petals as you add them to create a full bloom shape.

4 - Place a little glue in the heart of the flower, then add the final two petals from Step 2 for the finishing touch. Now, it's time to pair up the leaves. Dab a tiny bit of glue on the edge of one of the L-04 leaves and place the matching leaf on an angle, making sure the edges overlap a bit.

5 - Once your leaves are glued together, turn the flower upside down and adhere the leaves close to the edge of the bottom petal. You want to make the leaves peek out from the bloom if you intend to use these Rosettas as escort cards: That way, there will be enough room to write your guests' information on the leaves.

6 - With your flower still sitting upside down, dab a bit of glue in the center of the bottom and add the calyx on top of the leaves. Not only will this give your Rosetta a clean design, but the calyx will also help to keep the little leaves in place!

You may need to create a whole lot of these beauties, so repeat all the steps to make each one. Pro tip: Save some precious assembly time by pairing up the leaves ahead of time.

THE KARA

"When you look at the adjectives that pertain to a diamond—beautiful, strong, multi-faceted, unbreakable and brilliant, you see that they also represent women. We are taking the symbol of a diamond and having it represent women's strength." —Kara Ross

This beautiful flower came to life while I was working on a big exciting project. I named it after a lady whose passion for supporting and empowering women globally has touched millions of hearts, including mine!

. . . . .

Template P-04 x 3 (page 171)
Template P-24 x 4 (page 173)
Scissors or wooden stick
Hot glue gun and glue sticks
Curling tool
Template C-01 x 1 (optional, page 186)

1 - Once your petals are cut out, start by shaving each petal on the three P-04 templates with the edge of your scissors or a wooden stick. This motion will make the petals softly curl up toward the center of each layer.

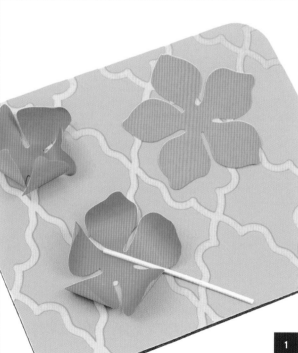

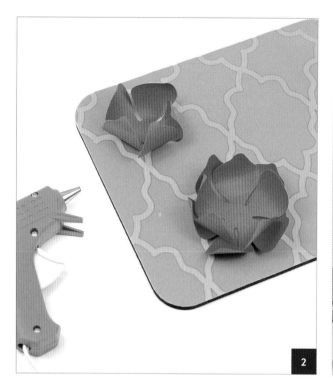

2 - Dab a bit of glue in the middle of one of the P-04 templates and add the other identical petals one at a time. Remember to add glue between each layer and stagger the petals as you stack them to create a full bloom.

3 - For the smaller petals (P-24), curl each individual petal tightly with the skinny part of your curling tool.

4 - Then, collapse each of the petals inward with your fingers to encourage a bud shape.

5 - Now dab a bit of glue inside one bud and nest each of the other three inside the first one, adding glue between each layer. This should create a tight, textured bud.

6 - Once completed, the finalized bud can be added to the heart of the bloom with a small dab of glue.

Repeat these easy steps three times to make a trio of fabulous Kara flowers! Follow the basic steps found on page 11 to mount the Kara on wire stems using template C-01 for the calyx.

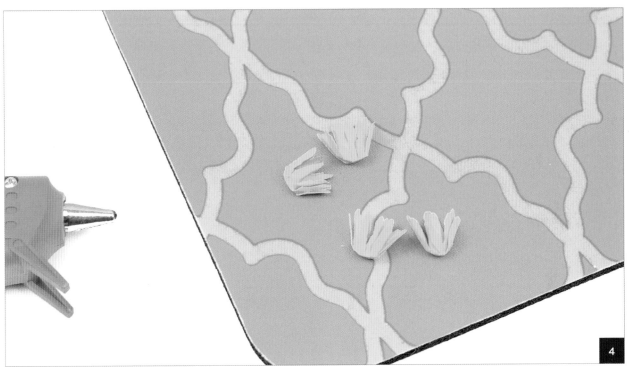

THE DARLING LADY

"She wore flowers in her hair and carried magic secrets in her eyes. She spoke to no one. She spent hours on the riverbank . . ." —Arundhati Roy

Here is another bloom that came straight out of my imagined happy place. It's a bloom that could not be more fitting of a utopia where everything, including the floral landscape, is perfect. The Darling Lady quickly became a favorite of mine to add a touch of glamour to my up-dos and, of course, to bouquets and centerpieces! It's simple yet elegant and looks fabulous in just about any color!

. . . . .

Template P-05 x 3 (page 171)
Template P-06 x 1 (page 171)
Template P-08 x 2 (page 171)
Curling tool
Molding mat
Dimensional tool
Hot glue gun and glue sticks
Felt pad
Hairpin
Template C-01 x 1 (optional, page 186)

1 - Once your petals and calyx are cut out, curl all three of the P-05 petals inward using your curling tool.

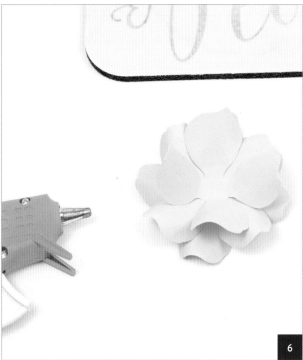

2 - Then, gently press the middle of each petal center into the molding mat with the help of your dimensional tool. Make sure that you do this step with the curls of the petals facing down.

3 - Next, it's time to curl the P-06 petal. Curl this petal a little differently: with one side of each individual petal facing down and one side facing up.

4 - Use your dimensional tool and molding mat to press the middle of the P-06 petal.

5 - Finally, curl each of the two small P-08 petals tightly inward.

6 - Now that all your petals are ready, use the glue gun to dab a small amount of glue in the center of the three P-05 petals with the curls facing down. Stack these petals, making sure to stagger the placement of each layer to create a nice full bloom.

7 - Add the P-06 petal to the center of the stack.

8 - To fashion the bud, nest the smaller (P-08) petals inside each other to create a bud shape. You'll want to secure each petal with a dab of glue as you go. Finally, glue the newly created double bud into the center of the stacked petals you previously prepared.

9 - To mount the bloom on the hairpin, start by adhering the felt pad to the surface of the pin with the glue gun and let it dry for a few minutes. Before adding the flower, I always pull lightly on the felt pad to make sure it's well adhered.

10 - Once I'm confident that it passes the test, I dab a fair amount of glue on the center of the felt pad and add the bloom. You'll want to keep pressing the flower to the felt for a few seconds while the glue dries.

If you wish to mount the bloom on a wire stem instead of a hairpin, follow the instructions found on page 11 of Basic Techniques using template C-01 for the calyx.

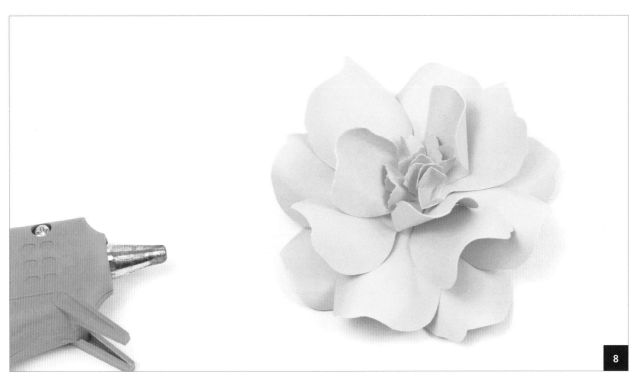

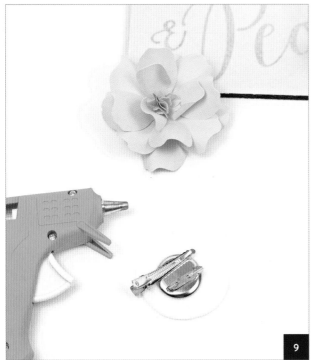

THE ANEMONE

When it comes to looking delicate and graceful, Anemone flowers are pros. These charming blooms have inspired poets, artists and songwriters for centuries with their colorful cup-shaped petals and contrasting dark or yellow centers.

The anemone flower's message is: Look forward to the future and don't forsake the ones you love. Something new is always around the corner, no matter how dark things might look right now (flowermeaning.com).

. . . . .

Template P-26 x 3 (page 172)
Template P-22 x 3 (page 175)
Curling tool
Dimensional tool
Molding mat
Hot glue gun and glue sticks
Template C-02 x 1 (optional, page 186)

1 - Once your petals are cut out, start by curling all the individual petals on the three P-26 templates inward using your curling tool.

2 - Then, using the dimensional tool, gently press the center of all the petals, with the curls facing up, into the molding mat.

3 - Dab a small amount of glue at the center of one of the P-26 petals, making sure its curls are facing up. Add the other two identical petals one at a time, dabbing some glue between each layer. Don't forget to stagger the petals as you stack them to create a dimensional effect.

4 - To prepare the stamen you will need your dimensional tool and the molding mat as your working surface. Apply light pressure to the middle of all three P-22 petals, creating a circular motion. The edge of the petals should curl up as you do this. Dab a little hot glue on the inside of two of the three P-22 petals and nest them inside each other with their petals facing up.

5 - To add the stamen to the bloom, dab a bit of glue at the bottom of the remaining lightly curled P-22 petal and place it at the heart of the large petal stack. It will act as a base.

6 - Add the squished stamen with a final dab of glue.

Repeat these easy steps twelve times to make a beautiful bouquet of Anemones. Refer to page 11 of Basic Techniques to mount the Anemone on a wire stem using template C-02 for the calyx.

THE SUCCULENT

In botany, succulent plants, also known as "succulents" or sometimes "fat plants" are considered unusual because of their abnormally thick and fleshy bits. The purpose of their plump leaves is to retain water—a useful feature in arid climates or dry soil conditions. I think they translate adorably to the paper flower world and are a lovely original choice of foliage for any arrangement. Given how cute they are, you may prefer to enjoy them in a more simple way: tucked in a little pot with just a touch of dry green moss.

. . . . .

Template P-01 x 2 (page 171)
Template P-02 x 1 (page 171)
Template P-19 x 1 (page 175)
Blending tool or sponge
Ink pad (darker shade of green or light brown)
Hot glue gun and glue sticks
Curling tool
Dimensional tool
Molding mat
Template C-03 x 1 (optional, page 186)

1 - Once your petals are cut out, first use the blending tool to lightly dab ink on the edges of both sides of all the petals.

2 - Once the ink is dry, you are ready to use your curling tool to curl the edges of the P-01 petals with one side facing up and one side facing down.

3 - Then, curl all the petals on template P-02 inward.

4 - Using your dimensional tool, press the middle of the petal gently into the molding mat, with the curls facing down.

5 - For the last little piece (P-19), softly curl the edges of the petal and press the middle of the center gently with curls facing up.

6 - Starting with one of the larger petals as the base, dab a little bit of glue and adhere the second large petal. Make sure to stagger the petal placement of these two large petals for the fullest effect.

7 - Then, glue the P-02 petal to the middle with the curls facing down.

8 - Lastly, add template P-19 to the stack with the curls facing up.

Follow the basic steps found on page 11 to mount the Succulent on short wire stems using template C-03 for the calyx. Repeat the steps three times to make a sweet mini potted Succulent arrangement.

2010 amy Mackiewicz

Thanks

THE WANTTOUBI ORCHID

The Wanttoubi (pronounced *Wawnt-tuh-bee*) Orchid comes directly from my imagination. But honestly, with over 25,000 species and over 100,000 varieties of orchids around the globe, the Wanttoubi Orchid might have a twin somewhere in the natural flower world.

While doing research about orchids, I learned so many interesting facts. Not only is their fragrance used in perfumes and beauty products, but the beans of the vanilla orchid are also used to flavor ice cream, soft drinks and cakes. No wonder vanilla is the second-most expensive spice after saffron!

· · · · ·

Template P-31 x 2 (page 174)
Template P-32 x 1 (page 175)
Template P-33 x 1 (page 174)
Ink pad and blending tool (choose a light color)
Fine-tip felt pen
Curling tool
Hot glue gun and glue sticks
Molding mat
Dimensional tool
Template C-03 x 1 (optional, page 186)

1 - Once your petals are cut out, use your sponge or blending tool to rub a little bit of ink on petal P-33.

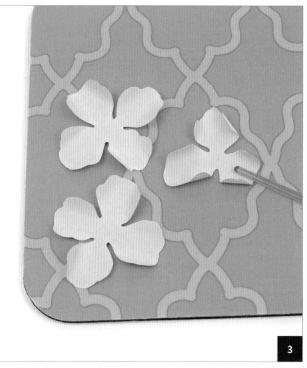

2 - Then, make tiny dots all over the petal with your fine-tip felt pen. Let dry.

3 - Gently curl all the edges of each individual petal on all templates inward with your curling tool.

4 - Next, lightly press the middle of each of the four petal centers into the molding mat with your dimensional tool. Make sure that the curls for petals P-31 are facing downward and that the curls for petals P-32 and P-33 are facing upward as you complete this step.

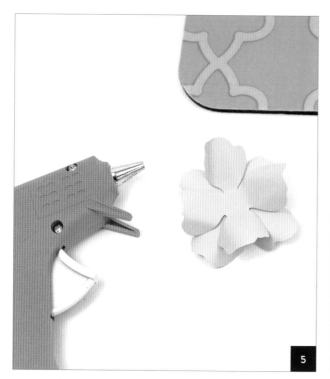

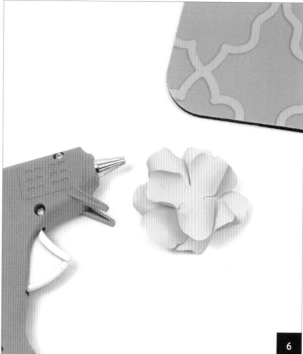

5 - It's time to assemble the orchid! Starting with the largest petals (P-31) as your base, dab a little glue in the middle of one petal and stack the other one on top with the curls facing down.

6 - Add petal P-32 with the curls facing up to the middle of the stack.

7 - Then, place the last piece (P-33) on top with its curls facing up.

To mount the Wanttoubi Orchid on short stems, cut the calyx (C-03) out of the same color as your orchid petals and refer to page 11 of Basic Techniques.

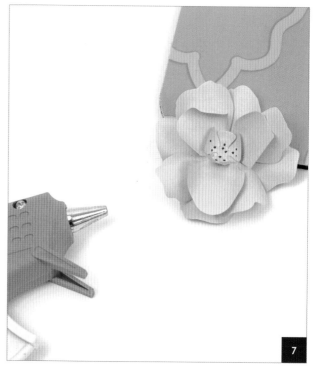

THE PAPERWHITES

Paperwhites are among the most popular flowering bulbs of the world for two apparent reasons: the beauty of their flowers and their exquisite fragrance. They are one of the smaller flowered *Narcissi* from *Jonquilla* cultivar variety. A personal favorite, the Paperwhite Narcissus resembles snow and is often associated with the month of December. The mounted stems in a little flowerpot makes for the perfect hostess gift!

. . . . .

Template P-02 x 1 (page 171)
Template P-34 x 1 (page 174, or a mini star shape punch)
Template P-35 x 1 (page 175, or a mini star shape punch)
Template C-03 x 1 (page 186, same color as the flower)
Template L-07 x 7 (page 187)
Curling tool
Needle-nose pliers
Dimensional tool

Molding mat
Hot glue gun and glue sticks
Wire stems (26 gauge)
Waterproof floral tape
Wire cutter
Floral foam
Dry green moss

1 - Start by cutting all your petals, calyx and leaves. As noted in the materials list, using very small paper shape punchers can save you a little time for this project, so feel free to sub them out for the P-34 and P-35 templates, if you wish. They come in handy to make smaller pieces, like those used for the stamen.

2 - To shape petal P-02, you'll need to curl each individual petal inward with your curling tool.

3 - Next, pinch and twist the tip of each petal with your needle-nose pliers or your fingernails to create the same natural effect as the real bloom.

4 - To prepare the stamen, apply light pressure to the middle of petal P-34 with your dimensional tool—the edge of the petals should curl up as you press the petal into your molding mat. Repeat this step with the mini star shape or petal P-35. The narrow tip of a chopstick will do the trick and make the edges of the star curl up.

5 - Dab a little hot glue on the bottom of petal P-34 and add it to the center of your larger petal shape P-02. Then, secure the yellow star inside with a little glue. Your flower is now done! To create a cluster of seven blooms, you'll need to repeat these steps seven times.

(continued)

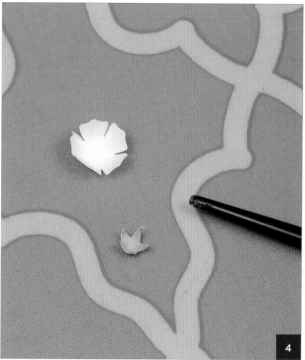

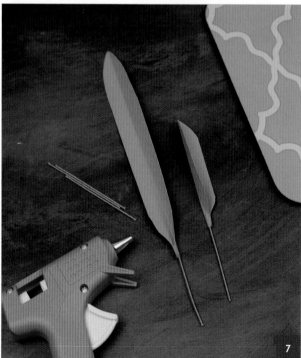

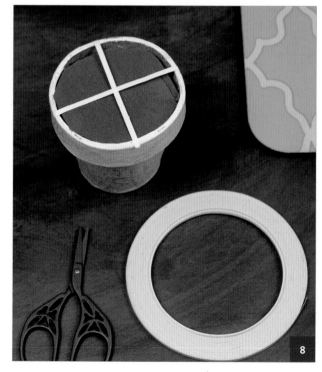

6 - Use calyx C-03 to mount each bloom on a wire. For the step by step guide on how do this and tips on how to wrap the stem with floral tape, refer to page 11 of Basic Techniques. Once mounted on stems, group your flowers into a bunch, using the floral tape to secure them together.

7 - Now it's time to add leaves and complete the flowering paperwhite bulb arrangement! Fold the leaves (L-07) in half and mount them on 2-inch (5-cm) tall wire stems. I like the look of varied leaf sizes in this case, so go ahead and cut your leaves to several lengths, some taller than the flowers and some shorter.

8 - Fill the inside of your container with floral foam and use the waterproof tape to secure it in place.

9 - Glue small pieces of green moss on top of the floral foam to hide it.

10 - Finally, it's time to anchor your cluster of seven blooms into the moss-covered foam and assemble your arrangement. Pro tip: By placing two of the tall leaves next to the flowers, you'll be able to hide the tape-covered wire.

THE CAMELLIA

When I think of the delicate camellia flower, femininity instantly comes to mind. For many, a tender quality found in a woman's appearance, manner and nature is synonymous with this gentle bloom. No wonder the camellia is one of the most instantly recognizable emblems in all of Chanel's accessories, clothing and jewelry collections! Coco Chanel first fell in love with the camellia after she read *La Dame aux Camélias*, a story by Alexandre Dumas in which the heroine always wore a white camellia, showing to the world that her heart remained pure. I often make the Camellia as a corsage or a brooch pin—a classy fashion accessory!

. . . . .

Template P-37 x 2 (page 174)
Template P-36 x 2 (page 175)
Template P-26 x 1 (page 172)
Template C-02 x 1 (page 186)
Dimensional tool
Molding mat
Hot glue gun and glue sticks
Scissors or wooden stick
Flat-back corsage pin

1 - Once your petals and calyx are cut out, prepare the stamen by applying light pressure to the middle of each P-37 petal with your dimensional tool, using a circular motion as you press into the molding mat. The edge of the petals should curl up as you roll the tool.

2 - Dab a little hot glue on the middle of these petals and nest them inside each other. The petals should be facing up. Then, gently press them inward with your fingers to form a little bud.

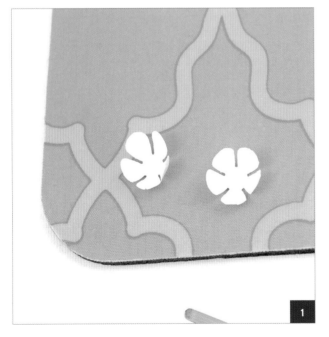

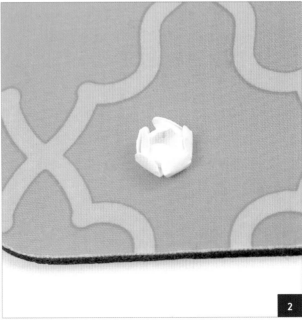

3 - Next, use your wooden stick or the blade of your scissors to gently shave petals P-36 and P-26. Make sure your shaving motion starts in the middle of the petals and carries through to the tip.

4 - Gently press the middle of each of the petals into the molding mat with your dimensional tool, with the curls facing down.

5 - Dab some glue in the center of one of the largest petals (P-36) and start building the bloom by adding the other P-36 petal followed by petal P-26, with the curls facing down. Don't forget to stagger the petals as you add them to the stack to create a dimensional effect.

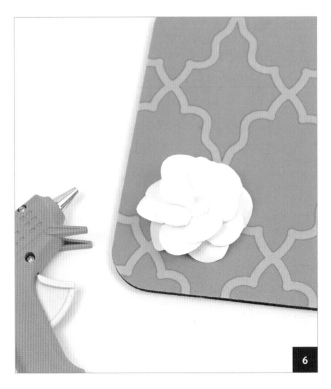

6 - Then, it's time to add the bud by dabbing a bit of glue to its base and placing it in the heart of the bloom.

7 - To mount the bloom on a flat-back corsage pin, simply dab a generous amount of glue to the back of the pin and place it on the middle of the calyx (C-02). Don't be afraid to add a bit of pressure to make sure the pin is well adhered to the calyx.

8 - Once the glue is dry, dab some glue on the calyx and place it under the camellia flower.

If you wish to mount the fabulous camellia flower on a stem instead of a pin, please refer to page 11 of the Basic Techniques section.

THE POMPOM CHRYSANTHEMUM

Given their happy look, it's no surprise that chrysanthemums symbolize optimism and joy. My version of the Chrysanthemum has a rock-n-roll twist to it. It's a little spiky and rebellious, which makes it the perfect choice for my alternative/offbeat style bouquets.

. . . . .

Template P-23 x 9 (page 174)

Curling tool

Scissors

Molding mat

Dimensional tool

Hot glue gun and glue sticks

Template C-03 x 1 (optional, page 186)

1 - First, cut out your petals. Then use the skinny part of your curling tool to achieve a tight curl on all P-23 petals.

2 - Now take three of the P-23 petals and modify them slightly by making a small cut going toward the center in between each individual petal. These cuts will allow you to close the petal layers into a tighter cluster at the heart of the bloom to create a full flower center.

3 - Next, using your molding mat as work surface, gently press the middle of each petal center with your dimensional tool. You'll want to complete this step with six of the P-23 petals with curls facing up, including the three modified ones.

4 - Then, take the three modified petals and squeeze them with your fingers to create a tight cone with the curls facing down.

5 - To assemble the flower, dab a small amount of glue in the center of the petal layers, making sure the curls are facing up, including the "squeezed" cones that you just prepared. Add the six P-23 petals you've worked on, one at a time, dabbing some glue between each layer. Don't forget to stagger the petals as you add them to the stack to create a dimensional effect.

6 - Lastly, turn the flower upside down and dab some glue in the middle. Place the three unused P-23 petals one on top of the other, one at a time. Make sure you do this with the curls facing the same direction as the already-glued ones.

7 - The newly added petals will create a draping skirt effect.

To mount the bloom on a stem, follow the steps found on page 11 of the Basic Techniques section. You will need template C-03 for the calyx. Repeat these easy steps three times to make a lovely trio of Pompom Chrysanthemum flowers.

THE DAISY

Daisies are what boho dreams are made of. They bring to mind sun-soaked wildflower fields, spontaneous wanderings in the country air, the simple joys of bundling found blooms and foliage into a worn basket. I can almost smell the sunshine when I look at these happy flowers and feel the urge to wear a flower crown and spin around barefoot! Daisies are the perfect addition to any laid-back and rustic décor or shabby chic event! Try them in a big bunch for a sunny display year-round.

. . . . .

Template P-23 x 3 (page 174)
Template P-22 x 3 (page 175)
Curling tool
Molding mat
Dimensional tool
Hot glue gun and glue sticks
Template C-02 x 1 (optional, page 186)

1 - Once your petals are cut out, use the narrow part of your curling tool to lightly curl each P-23 petal inward.

2 - Then, gently press the middle of each of the three petals into your molding mat with your dimensional tool to create a bit of dimension. The petals should be facing up.

3 - Now it's time to prepare the stamen. Using your dimensional tool and the molding mat as your working surface, apply a small amount of pressure to the middle of the three P-22 petals, all while moving your tool in a circular motion as you press. The edge of the petals should curl up as you roll the tool in this way.

4 - Dab a little hot glue on the inside of the three smallest petals (P-22) and nest them inside each other. The petals should be facing up. Now it's time to press them hard with your thumb as if you were squishing a bug! This will make the stamen look more natural. Dab glue in the center of the P-23 petals and layer them one on top of the other with the curls facing up, staggering each layer for a natural effect.

5 - Now add a bit of glue to the bottom of the stamen, then press it to the middle of the stack of daisy petals. You just made a fabulous little daisy!

Repeat these easy steps as many times as you want to make a bunch of daisies. Refer to page 11 for the basic steps to mount the daisy on a wire stem, using template C-02 for the calyx.

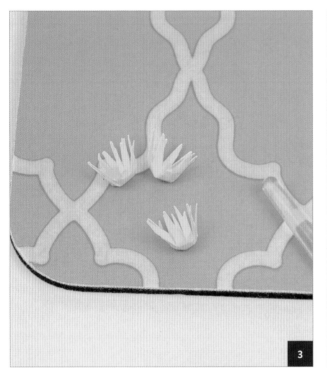

THE ORIENTAL POPPY

When I first saw the Oriental Poppy named Turkish Delight, I knew I had to design a similar paper flower to add to my collection! Would you believe that it can grow up to 30 inches (76 cm) tall and 6 inches (15 cm) in diameter? This delightful bloom is a total departure from the traditional poppy because of its size. I've enjoyed creating it in a variety of colors with fantastic results, and it looks especially smashing arranged as a seven-flower bouquet.

. . . . .

Template P-25 x 3 (page 173)
Template P-24 x 5 (page 173)
Curling tool
Molding mat
Dimensional tool
Hot glue gun and glue sticks
Template C-01 x 1 (optional, page 186)

1 - Once your petals are cut out, start by curling the three largest petals (P-25) with your curling tool, making sure to curl one side of each individual petal facing up and the other side facing down.

2 - Gently press the middle of the P-25 petals on the molding mat using your dimensional tool.

3 - Dab some glue in the center of one of the P-25 petals and start building the bloom by adding the other petals. Don't forget to stagger the petals as you add them to the stack to create a dimensional effect.

4 - Now it's time to prepare the stamen. Using your dimensional tool and the molding mat as your working surface, apply a small amount of pressure to the middle of the five P-24 petals, all while moving your tool in a circular motion as you press. The edge of the petals should curl up as you roll the tool in this way.

5 - Dab a little hot glue on the inside of the five P-24 petals and nest them inside each other one at a time to form a bud. The petals should be facing up as you do this. Once your bud is ready, it's time to press it with your fingers to make sure all the petals are tightly secured to each other.

6 - Next, add a bit of glue to the bottom of the bud and nestle it into the heart of the bloom.

Follow the basic steps found on page 11 to mount the Oriental Poppy on wire stems using template C-01 for the calyx. To make a full bouquet, repeat all these easy steps seven times.

CHAPTER TWO

Mini Blooms: The Fillers for Floral Arrangements

I love when my floral compositions look full and lush—which is where the mini blooms come in. The mini blooms are not only adorable, but they also fulfill two special functions. The first and most obvious one being that they are the perfect size to fill the gaps between the larger blooms in bouquets or centerpieces, making them more lush and textured. They are also a great way to add a subtle hit of color or sparkle.

THE BILLY

Inspired by the Billy Ball flower, also known as Craspedia, the Billy features a long, brilliant green stem on top of which rests a sphere-shaped bright yellow head. Although I often make this bloom in bright yellow, they are just as pretty in other fun colors.

. . . . .

Template P-08 x 8 (page 171)
Curling tool
Dimensional tool
Molding mat
Hot glue gun and glue sticks
Template C-03 (optional, page 186)

1 - Once your petals are cut out, start by curling the edges of all eight P-08 petals inward using the curling tool.

2 - Then, using the dimensional tool, gently press the center of all but three petals, with curls facing up, into the molding mat. The three remaining petals must be pressed with the curls facing downward.

3 - To assemble the Billy, start with one petal and dab a small amount of glue in its center, making sure the curls are facing up. Add one petal at a time, dabbing some glue between each layer. Don't forget to stagger the petals as you stack them to create a dimensional effect.

4 - For the last step, turn the Billy upside down and add the remaining petals to the base of the petal stack with the curls facing the same direction as all the other ones. This will create a lovely petal skirt effect.

Refer to page 11 for the basic steps to mount the Billy flower on a wire stem and use template C-03 for the calyx.

THE ZOYA

To all girly-girls out there, the Zoya, embellished with rhinestones or pearls, is the perfect mini bloom to add a fabulous sparkly effect to any floral composition!

. . . . .

Template P-37 x 3 (page 174)
Curling tool
Hot glue gun and glue sticks
Flat-back rhinestones or pearls
Template C-03 (optional, page 186)

1 - Once your petals are cut out, use the curling tool to curl the edge of all the petals inward.

2 - Then, using the dimensional tool, gently press the center of all the petals, with curls facing up, into the molding mat.

3 - Dab a small amount of glue in the center of one of the petals, making sure the curls are facing up. Add one petal at a time, dabbing some glue between each layer. Don't forget to stagger the petals as you stack them to create a dimensional effect.

4 - Dab some glue to your flat-back rhinestone or pearl and place it at the heart of your stacked petals.

Refer to page 11 for the basic steps to mount the Zoya flower on a wire stem and use template C-03 for the calyx.

THE ELLA

The sweet Ella flower is simple yet plays a big role in my floral compositions. Not only does it perfectly cover any gaps between the larger blooms, but the darker center also adds a touch of elegance and anchors the color palette together.

· · · · ·

Template P-09 x 1 (page 171)

Template P-38 x 3 (page 174, or a mini flower punch)

Scissors or wooden stick

Dimensional tool

Molding mat

Hot glue gun and glue sticks

Template C-03 (optional, page 186)

1 - Once your petals are cut out, use the edge of the scissor blade or a round wooden stick to shave all the individual P-09 petals, going from the middle to the tip.

2 - With the petals facing downward, apply light pressure to the middle of the petal layer with your dimensional tool, using your molding mat as a working surface.

3 - Repeat step 2 with the three P-38 mini flowers. The goal is for all the edges of the mini flowers to curl up.

4 - Dab a little hot glue on the bottom of the mini flowers and add them one by one to the center of the P-09 petal. You'll want to mind the placement of the minis so that they form a triangle shape at the center of the bloom.

Refer to page 11 for the basic steps to mount the Poppy flower on a wire stem and use template C-03 for the calyx.

THE TIA

This lovely bloom is my mini version of the Succulent (page 71). I often use green colored paper to make the Tia. There is no such thing as too much greenery in floral composition!

· · · · ·

Template P-02 x 2 (page 171)
Template P-39 x 1 (page 174)
Curling tool
Dimensional tool
Molding mat
Hot glue gun and glue sticks
Template C-03 (optional, page 186)

1 - Once your petals are cut out, curl each individual petal on all the petal templates inward with the curling tool.

2 - Next, using your dimensional tool and the molding mat as your working surface, apply light pressure to the middle of all the petal layers with the curls facing downward.

3 - To assemble the bloom, start with the larger (P-02) petals. Dab some glue at the heart of the petal and add the other matching one on top.

4 - Add glue to the bottom of the P-39 petal layer and add it to the heart of the bloom. Don't forget to stagger all the petals as you stack them for the best dimensional effect.

Refer to page 11 for the basic steps to mount the Tia flower on a wire stem and use template C-03 for the calyx.

THE MAYA

The Maya is my lovely cluster of mini blooms. In bunches of five, seven or even nine flowers, this bloom will add that extra texture to your floral arrangements!

. . . . .

Template P-02 x 2 (page 171)
Template P-18 x 1 (page 174)
Scissors or wooden stick
Hot glue gun and glue sticks
Curling tool
Template C-03 (optional, page 186)

1 - Once your petals are cut out, shave each P-02 petal upwards with the edge of your scissors or a wooden stick. This motion will make the petal softly curl up toward its center.

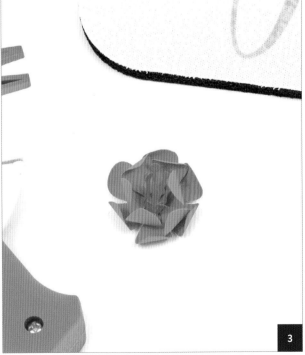

2 - Dab a bit of glue and stack the layers on top of the other, staggering them to create a full bloom.

3 - Now, squeeze the little petals of P-18 together with your fingers. Dab a bit of glue at the bottom and place it in the center of the larger petals.

Refer to page 11 for the basic steps to mount the Maya flower on a wire stem and use template C-03 for the calyx.

CHAPTER THREE

Oh-So-Fabulous Floral Arrangements

I love to create vibrant, whimsical floral compositions that are either executed with one single hue or the opposite—a blend of multiple colors!

In this chapter, we will be making nine different floral compositions and each has its own little thing going on. This is where you'll really see how imagination is crucial to designing fabulous floral arrangements!

One important point to remember when designing floral compositions: They should always *complement* the chosen color palette or environment in which they will be showcased.

Since all the bouquets I create are custom, I ask my clients to share a little bit about their occasion and the style of their event. Then, I choose flowers and colors accordingly. One important tip I've learned for selecting the right shade is that if you can't match a color perfectly, you should use it only as an accent. Trust me: If it doesn't match, it will clash! Focusing on a stunning complementary color instead of a close-but-not-quite-right one is one of the most helpful contributions you can make to the design.

FULL BLOOM—ALL ABOUT HUE

Green, orange, yellow and blue—each of these is a hue, a color or a shade. Keeping "hue" in mind, this fantastic project is to celebrate not only flowers but colors too! Since it's our first composition with the flowers you just learned to make, why not make it colorful and spectacular!

. . . . .

1 light pink Oriental Poppy (page 97)

2 coral Dahlias (page 31)

1 dark pink Peony (page 23)

2 light-purple Darling Lady flowers (page 61)

2 red Royal Roses (page 19)

2 orange Kara flowers (page 57)

3 white Daisies with yellow centers (page 93)

3 electric purple Anemones (page 67)

5 canary-yellow Billy flowers (page 102)

Mix of L-03 (page 187) and L-04 (page 187) leaves, mounted on stems

Floral tape

Ribbon

Narrow-opening vase

What an awesome list herein! Can you believe you have made all these blooms yourself? If the flowers are not already mounted on stems, do that now. Then we can start to arrange them! To make any floral arrangement, always start with the largest blooms. Here we have the Oriental Poppy and the Dahlias, so add those three in a triangle, and then add the Peony. Now go around and mix in the Darling Lady flowers, the Royal Roses and the Kara blooms. After that, mix in the smaller blooms like the Daisies, Anemones and the Billies. Add the leaves last to fill any remaining holes and add a touch of greenery throughout.

Secure the stems with floral tape before you wrap them with a lovely ribbon! Cut the stems to the desired length to fit into your narrow-opening vase.

DAISY AND FRIENDS

We've previously talked about the daisy as little free-spirited boho bloom, but the daisy also represents new beginnings. This is why they are often found in bouquets for new mothers or given as gifts to children. The daisy's thoughtful message is, ultimately, one of hope and renewal. If you are planning a baby shower, paper daisies arranged in a lovely teacup will make the perfect tabletop decoration!

· · · · ·

Up to 9 Daisies (page 93) mounted on short stems (the amount will depend on how wide the opening of your teacup is)
Template L-04 x 5 (page 187)
Template L-05 x 5 (page 186)
Floral foam
Teacup(s) and saucer(s)
Scissors or wooden stick
Corsage pins

First, prepare all of your daisies and leaves. Then, you'll need to cut the floral foam to fit your teacup. Once in place, secure it with the waterproof floral tape. I like to use this kind of tape because it's very sticky and holds the foam in place successfully.

If you can, use a lazy Susan as a working surface when you are assembling your arrangement. This way, you'll be able to quickly see every side of the project as you add the flowers.

It's time to work on all the L-04 and L-05 leaves. I like to give them a bit of texture by folding each leaf in half and slightly shaving the leaves to give them soft curves. This is easily accomplished with the edge of your scissor blade or a rounded wooden stick.

Using the corsage pins, spear some of the leaves into the foam all around the edge of the teacup. I've found that placing these bits of foliage ½ inch (4 cm) from the rim works well and allows the leaves to drape over the edge of the cup nicely.

Once you eyeball how many Daisies will fit in your teacup, insert the blooms into the foam. Remember to turn your Lazy Susan as you go to make sure the teacup is looking pretty from all sides!

Repeat these easy steps to fill as many teacups as your heart desires!

FIFTY SHADES OF PURPLE

Purple combines the calm stability of blue and the fierce energy of red. It's often associated with royalty, luxury, power and ambition. Purple also denotes wealth, extravagance, creativity, wisdom, dignity and independence. Talk about a meaningful shade! In fact, when I share photos of purple flowers on my social media channels, they're always a huge hit! If purple is *your* favorite color it says a lot about you too! Apparently, you are a sensitive and compassionate soul who generally thinks of others before yourself. This arrangement definitely makes the perfect gift for the purple-lover in your life!

. . . . .

2 medium-purple Oriental Poppies (page 97)

1 lilac Royal Rose (page 19)

1 dark-lilac Darling Lady (page 61)

1 medium-lilac Gardenia (page 27)

1 dark-purple Full Bloom Dahlia (page 35)

3 electric-purple Anemones (page 67)

3 violet Sophia flowers (page 39)

Template L-03 x 35 (page 187, using green crepe paper)

Wire stems

Wire cutters

Floral tape

Ribbon

Vase with a narrow opening

Mount all of the flowers on stems, if they aren't already.

We will also need to prepare some foliage for the bouquet. It will fill out the arrangement and add a lovely pop of complementary green. For this step, create three stems with five L-03 leaves on each, using green crepe paper. Simply follow the easy steps found on page 11 to make these—the same technique applies whether you're mounting one or multiple leaves on a wire stem.

Then, start assembling the bouquet in your hand by adding the Oriental Poppies, Royal Rose and Darling Lady blooms first. Next, fill in the gaps with the Gardenia, the Full Bloom Dahlia, the Anemones, the Sophia flowers and the leaf-only stems you prepared above. Feel free to adjust the placement of the different flowers so that you can enjoy the beautiful textures of this single-hue arrangement with maximum impact.

Once you are happy with the look of the bouquet, cut the stems with the wire cutter to the desired length and wrap the stems together securely with floral tape. For the perfect finishing touch, tie a ribbon around the stems and place them in a vase with a narrow opening.

PEONY CRUSH

If the Peony flower is not number one in your heart, I'm sure it's not too far down your list of favorite blooms! I love to display my paper peonies in short vases or couture gift bags. We won't mention any big names here, but if you follow me on Instagram or Facebook, you know who I'm talking about! *wink wink*

For this floral arrangement, I used a super cute little paper gift bag. The possibilities are endless here since these bags are available in just about any shade. You'll be able to make this design to complement various rooms or occasions!

· · · · ·

2 Peonies (page 23), mounted on short stems with leaves
Template L-03 x 7 (page 187, using green crepe paper)
Wire stems
Floral foam
Small paper gift bag

First prepare your peonies. Then cut your L-03 leaves out of green crepe paper and mount them on wire stems, per the instructions on page 11.

Cut a piece of floral foam that will fit inside your gift bag perfectly. This will help the bag maintain its shape and anchor the leaves and flowers in place.

Add the peonies to the bag, anchoring their stems in the foam. For a green finishing touch, add the leaves around the blooms to fill in any gaps.

RAY OF SUNSHINE

Bring on the citrus and sun with this stunning flower bouquet! The color yellow evokes positivity, warmth and happiness for most people. These decadent yellow flowers are sure to brighten anyone's mood and encourage joy throughout the day. As far as flowers go, these beautiful blooms are an absolute must for a gorgeous centerpiece in any space or home.

· · · · ·

1 white Gardenia with yellow ink (page 27)

2 light-yellow Kara flowers (page 57)

3 canary-yellow Billy blooms (page 102)

5 Zoya flowers, white with yellow centers (page 104)

Template L-06 x 3 (page 186)

Floral foam

Small flowerpot or container

Waterproof tape

Scissors

Corsage pins

Template L-04 x 3 (optional, page 187)

Hot glue gun and glue (optional)

First, prepare your flowers and leaves and mount the flowers on stems. Then, you'll need to cut the floral foam to fit your container. Once in place, secure it with the waterproof floral tape.

To shape the ferns, gently shave them with the blade of the scissors. This motion will give a soft curve to your leaves. Using the corsage pins, spear the three L-06 ferns into the foam around the edge of your container. Again, placing these bits of foliage ½ inch (1.5 cm) from the rim works well and allows the leaves to drape over the edge of your container nicely.

Anchor the flowers into the foam.

The other L-05 leaves can be glued directly to the bottom of the Gardenia flower if you wish to add more green!

THE BOOKWORM

"Bibliophile": a person who loves books. Someone who loves reading is also known as a "bookworm." Over the years I've had many clients describe themselves in this way to explain their requests for floral creations made from excerpts from their favorite titles. Projects rarely get more custom or personal than that! If you had to choose, which book would you pick to transform into a unique paper bloom?

. . . . .

5 Rose flowers (page 15), mounted on stems
Ink pad and blending tool or sponge (optional)
Floral tape
Ribbon (I love using vintage lace for this arrangement!)

As with any other paper flower you've learned how to make in this book, I suggest using 65-pound cardstock. You'll want to scan and print quotes or paragraphs from your favorite books on the cardstock for best results and follow the project steps for the Rose on page 15.

For this vintage look, I used parchment-textured paper and gave it an extra bit of old-world charm by distressing the edges of the petals with ink, just like we learned to do in the Succulent project on page 71.

Once your five Roses are ready and mounted on their stems, you can secure the bunch together with a bit of floral tape and add the perfect finishing touch: a ribbon made from vintage lace.

WHITE ON WHITE

The color white is a blank canvas just waiting to be written on. Compared to other more stimulating colors, it is a refreshing change, a soothing and calm visual experience for the mind, which allows for imagination growth and creativity. White contains a balance of all colors in the spectrum, representing both the positive and negative aspects of all colors. Given its properties and undeniable associations with purity, white tends to amplify and reflect other colors and textures. This is probably why I'm often asked to design white-on-white florals for marketing initiatives. The blooms add a delicate and feminine touch to the brand message, while allowing the product or idea to stand tall and look high-end.

Even though this arrangement is all white, the use of different flower styles creates visual interest and a rich texture.

· · · · ·

2 Dahlias (page 31)
3 Gardenias (page 27)
2 Camellias (page 85)
3 Full Bloom Dahlias (page 35)
2 Wanttoubi Orchid flowers (page 75)
5 Ella blooms (page 106)
Template L-04 x 5 (page 187)
Template L-06 x 4 (page 186)
White floral tape
White ribbon

Start by preparing and mounting all your flowers, leaves and ferns on their stems following the technique steps on page 11. For this design, use white floral tape and make sure all the calyxes are white, too.

Once your flowers and foliage are ready, begin assembling the bouquet. You'll want to include the larger flowers like the Dahlias and Gardenias first. Then, add the Camellias, the Full Bloom Dahlias and the Orchids. Next, evenly distribute the Ella blooms and the L-04 leaves throughout the arrangement. Lastly, surround the outside of the bouquet with those graceful ferns.

Secure your stems together in a bunch using white floral tape and cover the tape with your choice of white ribbon.

FERN ENVY

Let's talk about ferns! Everywhere I look I am seeing these graceful beauties more and more. They are a versatile star of the foliage world since they come in many shapes and sizes and add fantastic texture to most designs. Much folklore is associated with this plant too! A Slavic tale speaks of a fern that sadly bloomed only once a year but provided those lucky few who looked upon it with great happiness and many riches. Today, if you are giving someone a fern as a gift, you are also offering a symbol of hope, joy and security to the recipient. This is a great plant to give someone you really care about.

Ferns have been used in wedding bouquets since the early 1900s and were especially popular during the 1930s. Recently they've been making a comeback in all things wedding. It probably started with the surge in woodland/forest themes but has now been seen in just about any wedding style from woodsy to chic. When mixed with white flowers, it's an elegant and old-fashioned look, but when bunched on their own, they make a totally different but just as striking textural statement.

. . . . .

Template L-06 x 12 (page 186)

Wire stems

Hot glue gun and glue sticks

Waterproof floral tape

Floral foam

Small container

Dry green moss

This arrangement looks even more fantastic when you use different-size ferns. For an easy hack, I suggest scanning my L-06 fern template (page 186) and increasing or decreasing the size of the templates from 10 inches (25 cm) to 4 inches (10 cm) before printing them. This will help you trace the Fern at different scales.

Once all twelve ferns are cut, it's time to secure each of them to its wire stem. This step is easy, but you must work fast as the glue dries very quickly. Add a thin line of glue along the middle of the back of the fern, only from the middle to the bottom of the leaf. Then, place the wire on top. A small strip of green floral tape will help to cover the wire, but don't be afraid to add more glue to keep the tape in place if you feel it needs further securing.

Cut the floral foam to fit the inside of your container and use the waterproof tape to secure the foam inside. Glue small pieces of green moss on top of the floral foam to hide it. After you've shaped some of your ferns, it's time to anchor them into the moss-covered foam and assemble your arrangement. Voilà! Your fabulous potted fern should now look so lifelike that many will be doing a double take!

ALL ABOUT BERRIES

I'm sure you've noticed the silver brunia berry trend by now—they've been popping up everywhere from bouquets to boutonnieres recently. The silver brunia has a unique silver-gray hue that is hard to find in fresh flower products and adds a classic antique flair to any arrangement. They look gorgeous with everything from garden roses to soft dusty millers and succulents. What a chic way to add whimsy to a traditional centerpiece! When I first included these fascinating little berries in my bouquets, I had no idea how many requests for them would follow. They sure add a unique twist to any floral design!

• • • • •

Mini styrofoam balls (1-inch [2.5 cm] or smaller)

Corsage pin

Bare wire stems

Chalk paint in the vintage color of your choosing (I recommend blue gray or light gray)

Foam paint dabber

Floral tape

3 white Oriental Poppies with pink ink and dark-gray centers (page 97)

3 white Gardenias with pink ink (page 27)

3 green Succulents distressed with dark-gray ink (page 71)

5 ice-blue Anemones with dark-gray centers (page 67)

5 blush-pink Ella blooms with clear flat-back rhinestones (page 106)

Ribbon

To make a berry, start by piercing the styrofoam ball with a corsage pin. The little opening you'll create will make it easier to skewer the wire stem through the foam. Spear each ball with a bare wire stem to make individual berries. This is the same technique you would use to assemble a calyx (page 11): the coil on top will make the berry stay in place with very little glue.

When you have all your styrofoam balls mounted on stems, it's time to add color and transform them into berries! I recommend using chalk paint for this project since it dries with a very pretty texture that's almost identical to the real silver brunia—especially when you apply a thick layer with a foam paint dabber.

Once all your balls are painted and completely dried, group your berries in groups of three to five, depending on how big you wish the clusters to be. My preference is to make smaller clusters (three berries) and simply add more of them around the bouquet! Using the floral tape, secure the stems of your clusters together. Tip: Adjust the height of the berries in each bunch by sliding the stems to the desired position prior to taping—this will create a natural effect.

After you've prepared all the berry clusters, it's time to assemble the bouquet. Make sure to mount the blooms on stems if they aren't already. Start adding the blooms in the following order, largest to smallest: the Oriental Poppies, the Gardenias, the Succulents, the ice-blue Anemones and finally the Ella blooms. When you have all the flowers in place, add the berry clusters to the arrangement. Secure the bouquet with floral tape and cover it with a beautiful ribbon in a complementary shade!

CHAPTER FOUR

Forever in Bloom at Home

Throughout this book, you'll see me bring up the notion that "everyone loves flowers." To celebrate special days, brighten difficult ones, liven up a room or put an instant smile on your face, there's no easier gift.

Unfortunately, the beauty of real flowers is fleeting. They'll quickly start to wilt and die, leaving you with no option but to throw them away. That seems like such a shame and is so easily avoidable with everlasting paper flowers! There are so many ways to enjoy forever blooms in your home, beyond having them arranged in a vase. Check out these other ideas for adding a lovely floral accent to your home.

THE LAMPSHADE

A lampshade embellishment was one of the first DIY projects I tried with paper flowers in my own home. I still love the look of it! Not only is it very easy to execute, but it also makes for a pretty decor detail in any little princess's room!

. . . . .

Lampshade
10–20 stemless Darling Lady flowers (page 61)
Hot glue gun and glue sticks
Templates L-04 (page 187) and L-05 (page 186) as needed

I prefer to use a fabric lampshade for this purpose because, in my experience, the hot glue adheres very well.

The quantity of flowers and leaves needed will depend on the perimeter of your lampshade. For this project, the diameter at the bottom of my lampshade measured 10 inches (25 cm), and for that size I needed ten Darling Lady flowers.

Dab a bit of glue on the bottom of the flowers, press them firmly onto the lampshade and hold them in place for a few seconds or until you feel the flower is well secured to the fabric. Repeat this step until the bottom edge of the lampshade is fully covered with flowers.

Add the leaves here and there, to your liking, to create a lush visual effect.

THE TRINKET BOX

Trinket boxes come in handy and have many uses. Their purpose is to house little things that are precious or sentimental in nature, with the intention of keeping the chosen mementos in pristine condition. It's the perfect spot to tuck away jewelry, keepsakes, delicate gifts or odds and ends.

You can make and embellish your very own decorative boxes with chalk paint, glitter and, of course, paper flowers!

. . . . .

Papier-mâché trinket box (or any little container you have at home)

Chalk paint

Sponge

Hot glue gun and glue sticks

Template L-04 (page 187) as needed

1 stemless Gardenia (page 27, or another large bloom of your choosing)

Skinny strips of cardstock

Wooden stick

Start by painting your trinket box inside and out with chalk paint, using the sponge. Let dry.

To embellish the cover, dab a bit of glue on the bottom edge of the L-04 leaves and adhere them to the box. I like placing the leaves toward the middle and arranging them so that they drape over the edge of the box. Position the flower on top of the leaves and secure it with a bit of hot glue.

Shave the long, skinny strips of cardstock with your wooden stick to encourage them to curl. The shorter the shaving stroke, the tighter your curl will be.

Add one or two of these curly strips around the flower and secure with hot glue. Voilà! Your fabulous trinket box is ready to hold your precious treasures!

THE WREATH

I find the wreath to be a beautiful and effective way to add a bit of paper flower beauty just about anywhere. It's especially effective on a door, but think about using it in unexpected ways too—for instance, as a centerpiece.

My first wreath design was for a friend's wedding. Her venue included tall chandeliers at each table, which meant that a typical centerpiece would not work. Small wreaths that could sit at the base of the chandeliers added a pop of color and texture to her décor, without overwhelming or crowding the table. It was the perfect floral solution.

. . . . .

6-inch (15-cm) diameter grapevine wreath

Mix of stemless Marigolds (page 49), Succulents (page 71) and Daisies (page 93) in the color(s) of your choosing

Plenty of leaves (template L-04, page 187) and ferns (template L-06, page 186)

Hot glue gun and glue sticks

To adhere the flowers to the wreath, dab a bit of glue on the base of each bloom and add them one at a time. Note that the small marigolds are made with 4 P-21 templates (page 172) and 2 P-22 templates (page 175).

Once the whole ring is evenly covered with flowers, add the leaves to create texture and fill in any gaps. And that's it! Not only is this project beautiful, but it's so simple to make! Enjoy!

THE CANVAS

A blank canvas provides the artist in you with the perfect opportunity to express yourself!

There is absolutely no limit to what you can create. To execute an artful tableau, all you need is a willingness to experiment with paper flower crafts. Whether your goal is to make something beautiful, funky or eye-catching, give it a shot! I chose a timeless tone-on-tone look for this particular project, but feel free to have fun with the placement of the blooms or inject some color into your design!

. . . . .

Blank canvas

Pencil

Hot glue gun and glue sticks

9 Gardenias (page 27)

5 Pompom Chrysanthemums (page 89)

Plenty of white paper leaves (template L-04, page 187) and ferns (template L-06, page 186)

Prepare the canvas by identifying the desired position of your flowers with a pencil. Then, dab a bit of glue on the bottom of each flower and secure it to your canvas.

Lastly, add the leaves and ferns as desired to create texture and fill in any gaps.

The canvas can be mounted on a wall just like a painting or can be propped up on a shelf or table as a fabulous addition to any vignette.

THE GARLAND

It's exciting to see paper flower art taking on new styles, and the garland is one of my favorite recent examples. It's been a growing trend on the party scene, and it's a really fantastic way to jazz up your party's décor. Garlands are inexpensive, easy to make and have a big visual impact. This garland will go with a variety of décors!

· · · · ·

Ribbon
Hot glue gun and glue sticks
15 stemless Oriental Poppies (page 97)
Template L-05 x 30 (page 186)

To make five garlands, start by cutting five identical 4-foot (1.2-m) long strips of ribbon.

Make a little loop at one end of each ribbon and secure it with a bit of hot glue. This loop will help you hang the garlands and allow you to easily repurpose and relocate them after your event. (Hint: They look very pretty hung on a tree branch above a bed!)

Prepare your blooms and your leaves.

With the help of hot glue, adhere the leaves to the back of the flowers. Then, starting from the top* of the ribbon, place the flowers 4 inches (10 cm) apart. Now your garlands are ready to install onto your surface!

*To create visual interest, I started the bloom placement 4 inches (10 cm) from the top on two of the five garlands.

CHAPTER FIVE

Parties and Events with Paper Flowers!

Creating a truly memorable event is always a challenge. Whether it's a wedding reception, tea party, shower or intimate dinner at home with friends, the key to an unforgettable celebration is careful planning and details, details, details!

The first step in any event preparation is determining the purpose of the gathering and what you hope your guests will get from the experience. Next, sit down and create a design plan for your event—from start to finish. Brainstorm ideas for the theme, décor, menu and any other unique elements that will guide the style of your celebration. I always recommend developing a detailed timeline that covers everything from choosing a date, finalizing the guest list, narrowing down the event location, developing the budget and also little details like how you plan to greet guests or serve a particular course during the meal, for example.

INTIMATE DINNER PARTY

There's something special about gathering a few favorite people for a meal. A beautifully set table is the perfect canvas for a delicious meal. It won't come as much of a surprise that I love making paper flowers for my dinner parties and creating small centerpieces that complement my table linens and china.

If you are making floral centerpieces, the rule of thumb is to keep them low enough that guests can talk over them. I also love a candlelit table. Stick to unscented candles for these occasions; you don't want to interfere with the tastes and smells of your meal.

Assigned seating certainly isn't a requirement these days, but it can help the conversation flow more effortlessly at parties. Plus, it's an opportunity to craft some sweet paper flower place cards to complement the table setting. I just know your guests will be thrilled to bring their flowers home as keepsakes!

TEA PARTY

Tea parties became a popular social event in the early 1800s. To this day, they remain an enjoyable and popular pastime. Tea is, of course, necessary for tea parties, but often, small snacks are served as well.

Decorating the setting for this event is key to making it memorable. Since you can now make your own fabulous paper flowers, there's no need to make a trip to the florist!

A couple of simple bouquets on the tables is enough, but why not go the extra mile and greet your guests with beautiful flower corsages too?

BRIDAL SHOWER

A bridal shower is a fun, celebratory occasion that allows the bride's close friends and family members to spend time together before the big day. It's also practical in nature, as guests "shower" the bride-to-be with gifts to help her start a home with her future spouse.

As with other pre-wedding events, the guest list should be limited to people who are also invited to the wedding. For the bridal shower, this usually includes the bridal party, the bride and groom's mothers and sisters, aunts, close female cousins and grandmothers.

Eating, chatting and gift opening are primary shower activities. You'll also want to have background music (in keeping with the theme, if appropriate) and a few planned activities (simple games will do). You can plan anything from a barbecue in someone's backyard to an afternoon at a spa—think about what type of event the bride would enjoy the most.

You'll want to give the guests a token of appreciation for coming to the shower (and for bringing a gift). It doesn't have to be extravagant, but you can get creative with the presentation by utilizing beautiful Trinket Boxes (page 135) embellished with fabulous paper flowers!

TABLE NUMBER CARDS

Table numbers are necessary if you are hosting a large event with multiple tables—but their utilitarian purpose doesn't mean they can't also be a stylish addition to your tables! One important thing to keep in mind when designing table number cards is that the number itself needs to grab the guests' attention.

· · · · ·

Rosetta flowers (page 53)
Maya flowers (page 110)
Template L-04 scaled to different sizes (2 large and 1 small per card, page 187)
Hot glue gun and glue sticks
Table numbers printed on heavy (110-lb) cardstock

Once all your flowers are ready and their leaves have been texturized, it's time to add them to the cards.

Dab a bit of glue on the bottom of the leaves and place three of them on an upper corner of the printed table number card. Then, dab hot glue on the bottom of the Rosetta flower and place it on top of the leaves. Finally, add the Maya bloom tightly next to the Rosetta.

Repeat these easy steps for each of the cards needed for your event!

LOVE LETTERS

Decorating with large-scale letters at events or in the home has become a big trend lately. It's a brilliant way of customizing any space without making it look and feel *too* personal. The letters can be a nod to a last name or someone's initials or can form words of all kinds. It's truly a versatile décor tool! Customize these "love" letters to complement your event's theme and color palette!

· · · · ·

Papier-mâché block letters
Chalk paint
Sponge brush
Mix of stemless paper flowers (quantity depends on the size of your letters)
Plenty of paper leaves (template L-04, page 186) and ferns (template L-06, page 186)
Hot glue gun and glue sticks

Start by painting the letters in a complementary color with the sponge brush, covering the surface on all sides.

While the chalk paint dries, make all the paper flowers and foliage in a variety of sizes.

Once the paint is completely dry, adhere the flowers to the letters by dabbing a bit of hot glue at the base of each bloom. Now that all your letters are fully covered with flowers, it's time to add the leaves and ferns to introduce some extra texture. The letters can look lovely sitting on a shelf or table or hung on a wall!

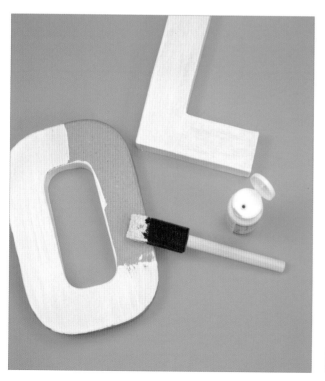

PLACE CARDS

A place card not only directs guests to the table where they will sit during the reception, but it also lets them know which spot is theirs at the table. They can be made to complement your menu cards and table number cards.

. . . . .

Rosetta blooms (page 53)
Template L-04 (page 187)
Hot glue gun and glue sticks
Printed name cards (3.5" x 1.5" [9 cm x 4 cm])

To make this Rosetta, which measures 2.75 inches (7 cm) in diameter, follow the instructions found on page 53, but use template P-20 instead of P-21. Make sure to add the L-04 leaves to the base of the bloom once it is ready.

Then, simply slide the printed name cards between two petal layers of the Rosetta bloom.

For a personal touch at a wedding, you can add a little round label with the name of the happy couple and the wedding date to the bottom of the flowers. The flowers will be a lovely keepsake for your guests.

CENTERPIECES

Paper floral centerpieces are perfect if you wish to add color and texture to your table. I like to use flowers that complement the napkin ring or place card holders.

. . . . .

Floral foam
Container
Waterproof floral tape
Corsage pins
5 Royal Roses on short stems (page 19)
Ferns (template L-06, page 186) and leaves (template L-04, page 187)

Cut the floral foam to fit inside your container and use waterproof floral tape to secure the foam inside.

Using the corsage pins, spear the L-06 ferns into the foam around the edge of your container. Placing these bits of foliage ½ inch (1.5 cm) from the rim works well and allows the leaves to drape over the edge of your container nicely.

Anchor the flowers that are already mounted on stems into the foam. Glue other leaves or ferns directly to the bottom of the Royal Roses if you wish to add more green!

FAVOR BOXES

The intention of party favors is to provide guests with a token of thanks for attending your event. The favor can be any take-home memento appropriate for the occasion. Jazzing up a favor box is easy: Simply adorn it with a beautiful handmade paper flower.

. . . . .

Favor box
Glue dot or double-sided tape
1 Rosetta flower (page 53)
Template L-04 (page 187)

Once you have filled your favor box with your item(s), place a glue dot or double-sided tape on top of the lid and secure your bloom in place.

Add a few leaves to the base of your bloom, as desired.

To create visual interest on the favor table, you might like to opt for Rosetta flowers in various shades of pink instead of making them all identical.

THE NAPKIN RING

Napkin rings are a pretty part of a complete place setting at any table. Their purpose is to secure a clean, folded napkin neatly until the diner is ready to use it. There are several different types of napkin rings and many different styles to accommodate place settings ranging from casual to formal. Why not add flair to your table with a surprising napkin ring design for your next dinner party?

. . . . .

Linen or paper napkin
Paper band (7" x 1.5" [18 cm x 4 cm])
Glue dots
Royal Rose flower (page 19)

Fold or roll the napkins to get them ready for assembly.

Wrap a paper band around the napkin and add a glue dot where the two ends meet.

Once the band is in place, add a glue dot to the bottom of a Royal Rose and place the flower on the middle of each band, strategically, to hide the seam.

Voilà! You've made a fabulous napkin ring and you can make as many as you will need for your next intimate dinner party.

CAKE FLOWERS

Paper flowers have taken the cake-decorating world by storm. They are absolutely perfect for those who want a fancy and unique-looking dessert. Plus, they look equally lovely on homemade cupcakes or store-bought sweets—a total win! This project is a great little hack to get the look of fresh blooms or fondant adornment at a fraction of the cost.

. . . . .

Grapevine wreath 4 inches (10 cm) in diameter

Hot glue gun and glue sticks

1 Gardenia flower (page 27)

1 Dahlia flower (page 31)

1 Royal Rose flower (page 19)

2 Maya flowers (page 110)

Plenty of leaves (template L-04, page 187) and ferns (template L-06, page 186)

To assemble this fabulous cake topper, start by fastening the Gardenia flower to the wreath by adding a generous amount of glue. Hold it in place until the glue dries or until the flower is firmly secured to the wreath.

Repeat the same steps for all the other flowers except for one of the Maya blooms.

Add the leaves and ferns to your design, filling in the gaps between the flowers. Next, add the remaining Maya bloom to the middle of one of the ferns.

MENU CARDS

According to wedding experts on the Emmaline Bride website, if your reception dinner is a sit-down affair, a menu card will let your guests know what is coming up next. (And help them anticipate allergy issues, if they are aware of the ingredients ahead of time.) Not to mention, a pretty menu card is a nice detail to include at each guest's place setting. They are just as appreciated at an intimate dinner party as at a larger event like a bridal shower.

. . . . .

Ribbon
Printed menu card (8" x 5" [20 cm x 13 cm], 65-lb cardstock recommended)
Hot glue gun and glue sticks
Cardstock for the base of the menu card (9" x 6" [23 cm x 15 cm], 110 lb recommended)
Rosetta flower (page 53)

Wrap the ribbon around the printed menu card and secure it with a bit of hot glue. Then, dab hot glue on the back of the menu card and place it in the middle the larger "base" card.

Dab hot glue on the bottom of the Rosetta flower and secure it to the middle of the ribbon on the card.

Repeat these easy steps to make as many menu cards as needed for your event.

CHAPTER SIX

Jaw-Dropping Backdrop

From wedding ceremonies to graduation parties, large paper flowers embellish any space with a wow factor that your guests are sure to remember. I've honestly lost count of how many large paper flower backdrops I've designed over the years—people just go crazy for them! One thing's for sure: It's a trend that is not ready to fade away.

In this chapter, you'll learn how to make four different styles of large paper blooms. Given that the scale of the petal templates in this book is rather small, I recommend that you photocopy and enlarge the noted petal templates to fill an 8.5 x 11-inch (22 x 28-cm) sheet of 65-pound cardstock to create these backdrops.

COMING UP ROSES

Large paper roses have a timeless and elegant look and make for a classy large-scale design, especially when clustered in different sizes.

· · · · ·

The following templates enlarged to fit an 8.5" x 11" (22 x 28-cm) sheet:
- Template SP-01 x 15 (page 176)
- Template SP-02 x 4 (page 178)
- Template SP-03 x 1 (page 177)

Large curling tool

Hot glue gun and glue sticks

1 - Once the petals are prepared and cut out, curl all fifteen SP-01 petals with your curling tool, making sure to curl one side of each individual petal facing up and the other side facing down. You don't want the curls to be too tight, so a thicker curling tool, like a glue stick or wooden rod, works best.

2 - Next, it's time to modify the appearance of your SP-01 petals with the flaps on the bottom of the petals. You'll want five of them to lie almost flat against the backdrop, five others to curl up a bit and the last five to have a more dramatic inward curl. The deeper the overlap you create with the flaps, the more the petal will curl up and off the backdrop. With that in mind, glue the flaps of five SP-01 petals with a looser overlap (¼ inch [0.5 cm]). For the next five, you'll want a medium overlap (½ inch [1.3 cm]). The last five petals will require a tighter overlap (1 inch [2.5 cm]).

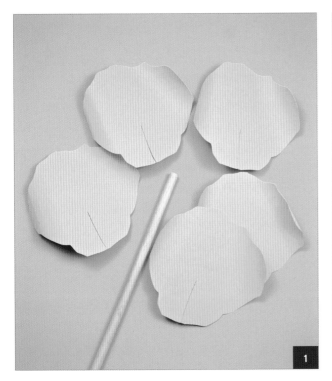

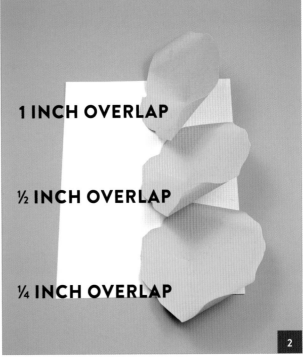

1 INCH OVERLAP

½ INCH OVERLAP

¼ INCH OVERLAP

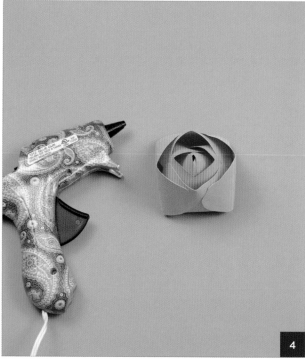

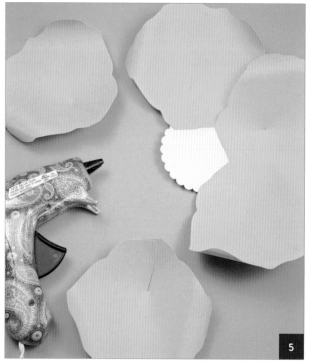

3 - To make the center of the bloom, start by forming a cone shape with two of the four SP-02 petals. Once the cone is tight, add glue to secure it in place. Dab a bit of glue to both corners of the third SP-02 petal and wrap it loosely around your cone.

4 - Repeat the same step with the fourth SP-02 petal. If you wish to make the cone larger, dab some glue on the bottom of the cone and secure it in the middle of your second SP-02 petal.

5 - Using template SP-03 as your base, glue the five flatter SP-01 petals along the edge of the circle.

6 - Repeat the same step this time with the five slightly more raised SP-01 petals—don't forget to stagger all the petals as you add them, to create a full bloom.

7 - Next, it's time to place three of the five remaining SP-01 petals. If you feel there is room, add the last two SP-01 petals to the bloom too.

8 - Finally, put a generous amount of glue at the base of your cone-shaped bud and place it at the heart of the bloom.

Repeat all these steps three times to make three large Coming Up Roses, or as many as you'd like!

OH! CAMELLIA

The large-scale Camellia adds a welcome softness to any floral backdrop. The heart of this flower also looks fabulous on its own! So, technically, this large Camellia can be used two ways.

. . . . .

The following templates enlarged to fit an 8.5" x 11" (22 x 28-cm) sheet:

Template SP-04 x 8 (page 179)
Template SP-05 x 4 (page 180)
Template SP-06 x 3 (page 181)
Template SP-07 x 3 (page 182)
Template SP-08 x 1 (page 177)

Curling tool

Hot glue gun and glue sticks

1 - Once your petals are prepared and cut out, start by shaping soft curls on each individual petal for templates SP-04 and SP-05.

2 - Next, it's time to modify the appearance of the SP-04 petals. You'll want them to lie flatter against the backdrop then the SP-05 petals. With that in mind, glue the flaps of the eight SP-04 petals with a looser overlap (¼ inch [0.5 cm]). For the four SP-05 petals, you'll want a bit more of an overlap (¾ inch [1.9 cm]). Remember, the deeper the overlap you create, the more the petal will curl up and off the backdrop.

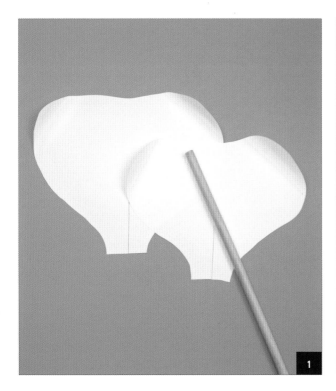

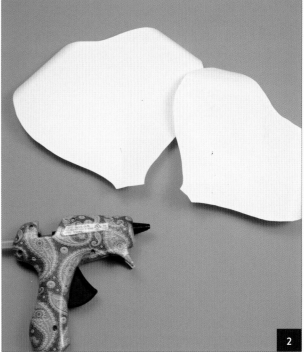

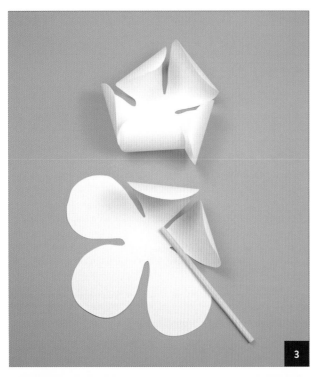

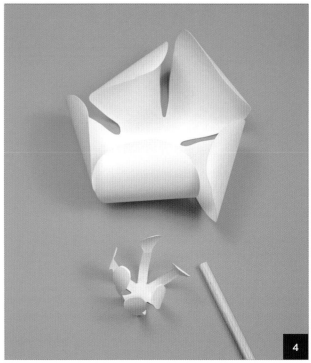

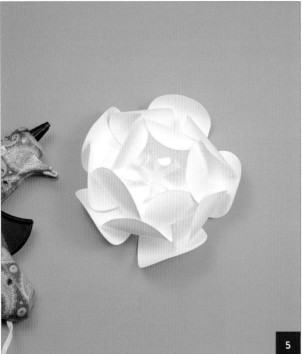

3 - To make the heart of the bloom, you'll need all three SP-06 petals. Shave the edges of all individual petals inward with your curling tool. Then, dab some hot glue and make sure to stagger the petal layers while placing them one inside the other, to create fullness.

4 - Next, you'll need to shave the individual petals of the three small SP-07 pistils so they all curl inward.

5 - Then, layer the SP-07 pistils one inside the other with a little glue between each layer. This will create a stack of pistils, which you can then place at the heart of the SP-06 petals prepared in step 3.

6 - To assemble the bloom, use the round SP-08 template as your base. Starting with the largest petals (SP-04), dab glue on the base of four of the petals and place them near the outside of the circle shape. Add four more of the SP-04 petals to create a second layer on top.

7 - With the remaining four SP-05 petals, create the third layer, staggering the placement of the petals so that all petals on the three layers are visible and create a full base.

8 - The finishing touch is adding the middle of the bloom. Dab a generous amount of hot glue in the bloom's heart, and place it at the center of your large petal stack.

Repeat these steps five times to make five large Camellias. Try a few blooms without petal SP-04 layers to make a few of the flowers smaller, for visual variety.

THE HIBISCUS

This fabulous Hibiscus wannabe is so simple to make but really packs a huge visual punch when used as a floral backdrop! It's the perfect choice if you are hosting a gathering with a tropical theme.

. . . . .

The following templates enlarged to fit an 8.5" x 11" (22-cm x 28-cm) sheet:

> Template SP-09 x 5 (page 183)
> Template SP-10 x 2 (page 182)
> Template SP-07 x 2 (page 182)
> Template SP-08 x 1 (page 177)

Bone folder
Hot glue gun and glue sticks
Curling tool

1 - Once your petals are prepared and cut out, fold all SP-09 petals along the middle of each petal using your bone folder to make the folds tight and crisp.

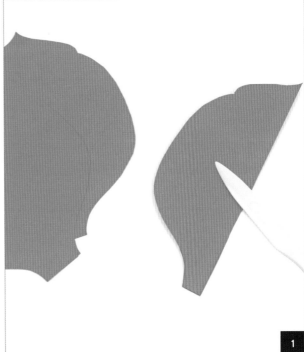

2 - Dab a bit of glue along the edge of the petal flaps and overlap the flaps by about ¾ inch (1.9 cm).

3 - Now, add a bit of pressure with your fingers and push each of the five petals down. The pressure and the way you've overlapped the petals will encourage the flower to curl into a natural shape.

4 - Use the round SP-08 template for your base and place the SP-09 petals you prepared above around the edge of the circle—the petal edges should overlap slightly.

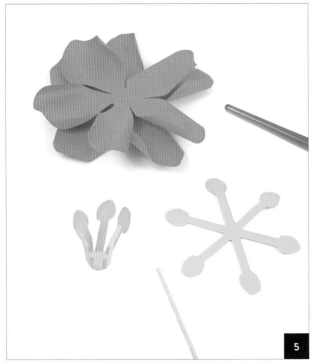

5 - To make the center of the bloom, curl both SP-10 petals, making sure to curl one side of each individual petal facing up and the other side facing down. Next, dab on a bit of glue and stack the SP-10 petals one inside the other. For both SP-07 templates, fold each individual petal inward at the edge of the heart of the template to create the pistil. This will make the pistil petals stand upright. Use glue to stack both pistils one inside the other.

6 - Dab some glue on the back of the stacked SP-10 petals and place it in the middle of the large SP-09 petal layer.

7 – Finally, dab some glue on the stacked pistils (SP-07) and place them in the middle of the SP-10 petals.

Repeat all these easy steps three times to make a trio of grand Hibiscus!

THE POPPY FIELD

The poppy is one happy bloom! What I especially love about this design is that the smaller petal templates can be blooms in their own right. So, you can make large and medium-size poppies using the same shapes.

. . . . .

The following templates enlarged to fit an 8.5" x 11" (22-cm x 28-cm) sheet:

- Template SP-11 x 6 (page 184)
- Template SP-01 x 3 (you'll need 6 if making a smaller poppy; page 176)
- Template SP-12 x 3 (page 185)
- Template SP-03 x 1 (page 177)

Curling tool
Hot glue gun and glue sticks

1 - Once your petals are prepared and cut out, curl all SP-11 and SP-01 petals with your curling tool, making sure to curl one side of each individual petal facing up and the other side facing down. You don't want the curls to be too tight, so a larger curling tool works best.

2 - Next, it's time to modify the appearance of the six SP-11 petals. You'll want them to lie flatter against the backdrop than the SP-01 petals. With that in mind, glue the flaps of the six SP-11 petals with a looser overlap (¼ inch [.5 cm]).

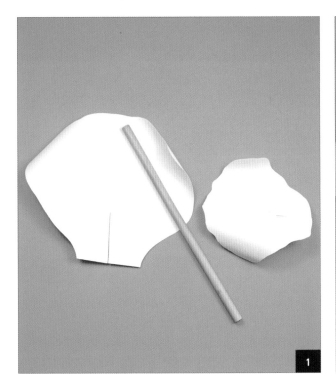

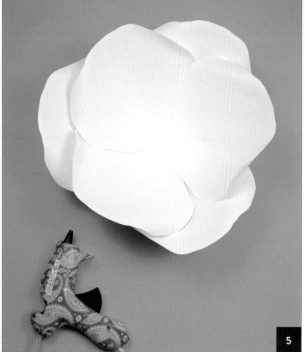

3 - For the three SP-01 petals, glue the flaps with a bit more of an overlap (½ inch [1.3 cm]). Remember, the deeper the overlap you create, the more the petal will curl up and off the backdrop.

4 - Using template SP-03 as your base, place three of the larger petals around the edge of the circle with a small dab of glue, keeping a small gap between each petal.

5 - Repeat the same step for the second layer of SP-11 petals.

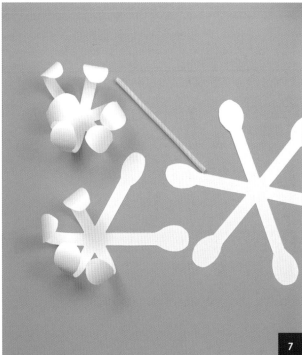

6 - Then, place the smaller petals (SP-01)—don't forget to stagger all the petals to create a full bloom.

7 - To make the center of your bloom, you'll need to prepare the SP-12 pistil petals on each of the three templates. To do so, shave all the individual petals toward the center of the template.

8 - Once all three SP-12 petals are ready, nest the petals inside each other, with a little glue between each layer. Finally, add the stacked pistil to the heart of your large Poppy bloom.

Repeat these easy steps five times to make five lovely Poppies!

LAYOUT AND ASSEMBLY TIPS

Mounting large paper flower backdrops onto a large surface is one of my favorite things to do!

Most of the time, I cannot affix the flowers directly onto the wall, so I use a very large canvas or Styrofoam panels. The Styrofoam panels are typically white and are 4 feet (1.2 m) wide, 8 feet (2.4 m) tall and about 1.5 to 2 inches (3.8 to 5 cm) thick. I usually cut them in half so they fit into my vehicle! You can find these boards at your local hardware store in the insulation section.

The first step is more of a planning one. I always decide on the placement of the flowers by moving them around on the board and settling on a final layout. Once I'm happy with how everything looks, I take a few reference photos. Don't skip this step—it will help you confirm that you have enough flowers to cover the whole surface nicely.

Then, if my working space allows for it, I like to arrange the boards (or canvases) in such a way that they are upright and facing me. Looking at the work from this angle as I go ensures that I cover all the gaps nicely.

Using a large glue gun and plenty of glue sticks, I then mount the flowers directly onto the boards. If you have multiple boards, try overlapping some of the flowers to cover up the seams in your design.

You'll find that adding plenty of foliage to your backdrop will help create a full and lush look and fill in the gaps between the big blooms. Don't be shy: use many! All the leaf and fern templates in this book can be enlarged to complement the scale of the flowers!

Voilà! You are now fully equipped with the easy steps to make fantastic paper flowers for all sorts of occasions. Have fun and don't forget to let your imagination go wild when playing with paper!

Oh! And please share your creations with me on Instagram or Facebook by tagging @paperandpeony or using the hashtag #PPforeverinbloom. I'd love to see what you come up with and bring attention to your designs too!

Templates

PETALS

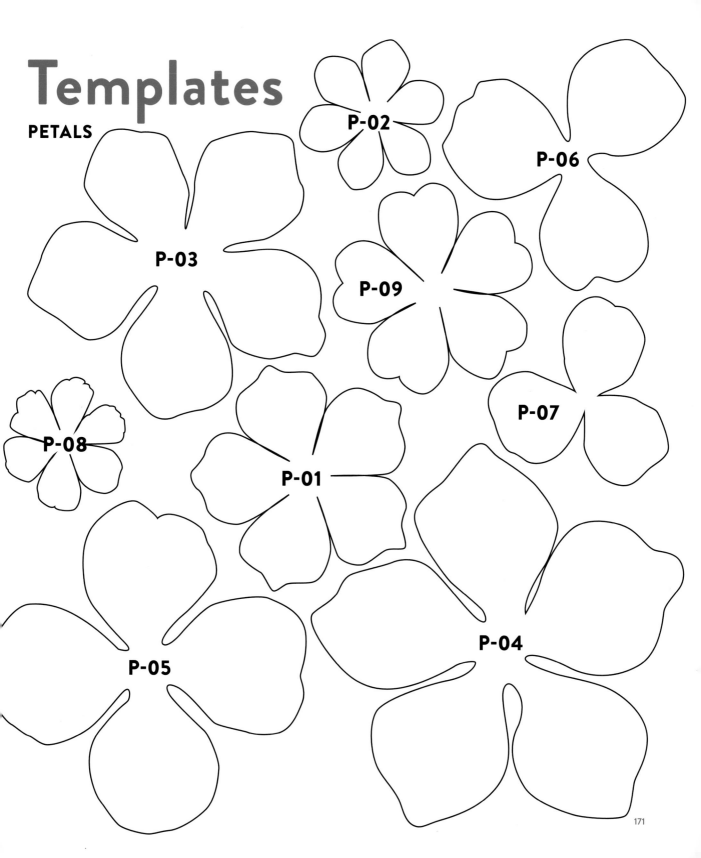

P-02

P-06

P-03

P-09

P-08

P-07

P-01

P-05

P-04

P-12

P-15

P-21

P-26

P-10

P-13

P-17

P-25

P-20

P-24

P-16

P-27

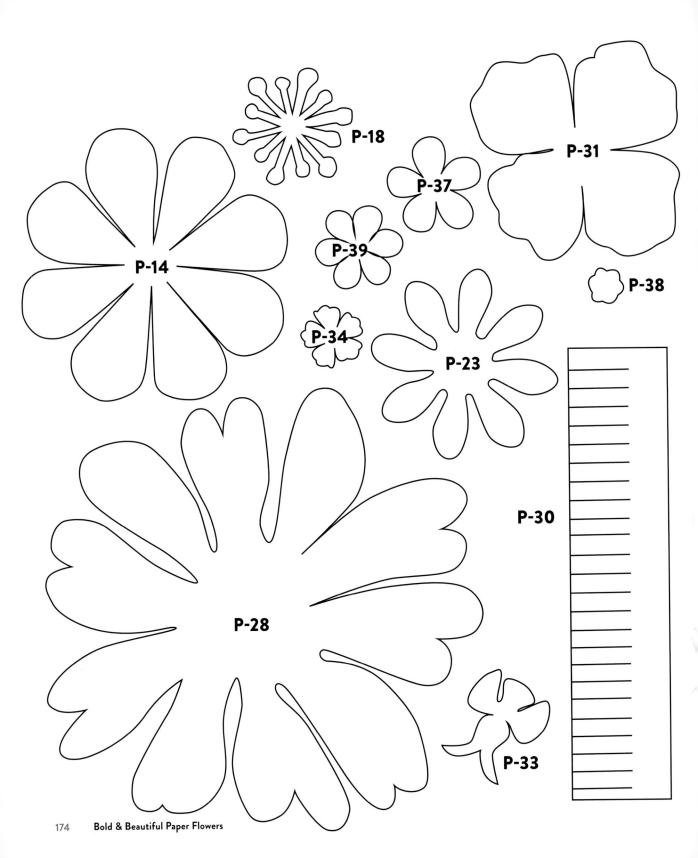

P-18

P-37

P-31

P-14

P-39

P-38

P-34

P-23

P-30

P-28

P-33

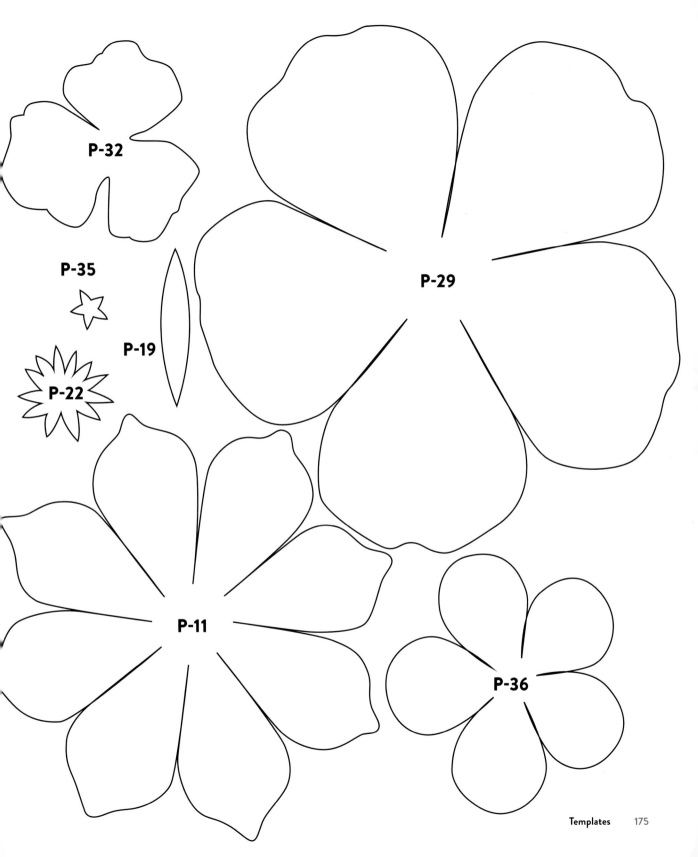

P-32

P-35

P-19

P-22

P-29

P-11

P-36

LARGE PETALS

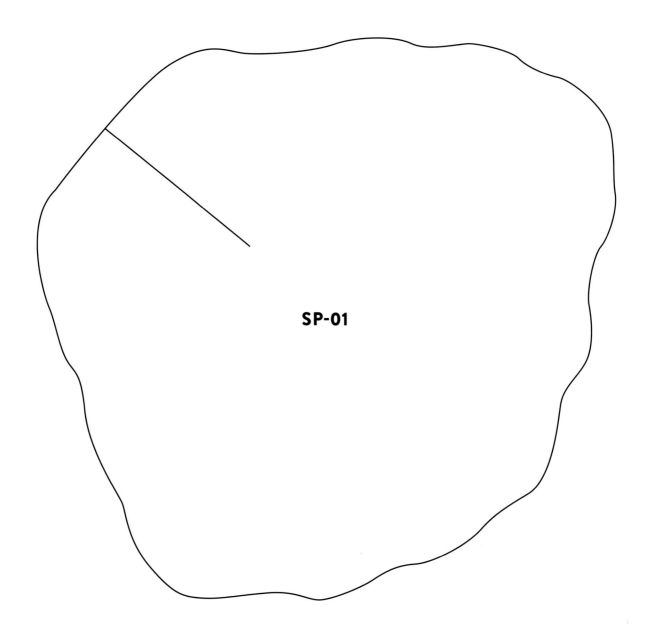

SP-01

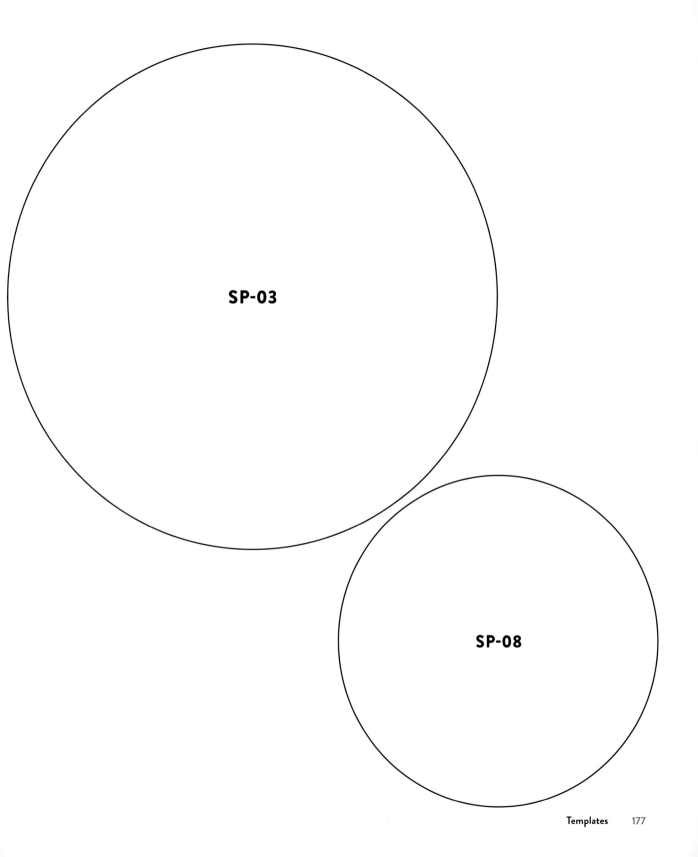

SP-03

SP-08

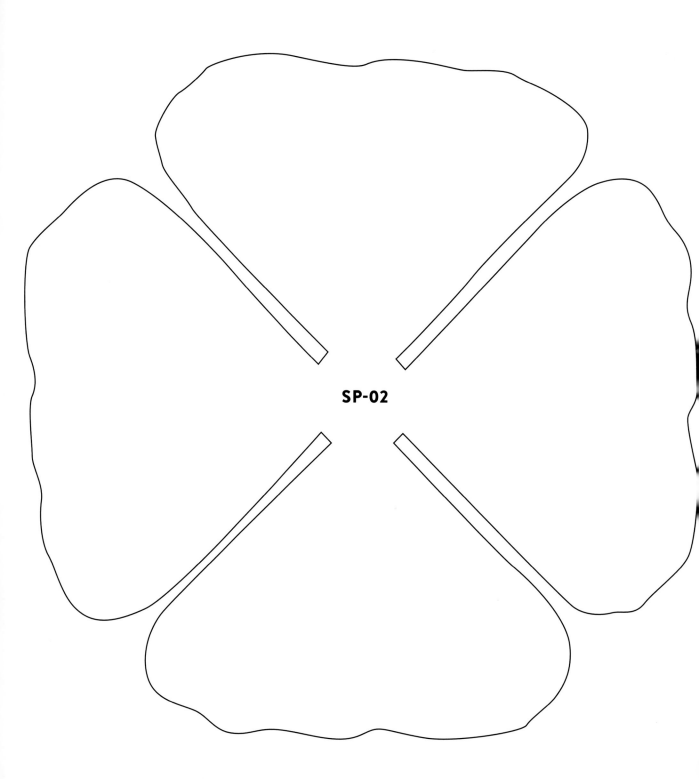

SP-02

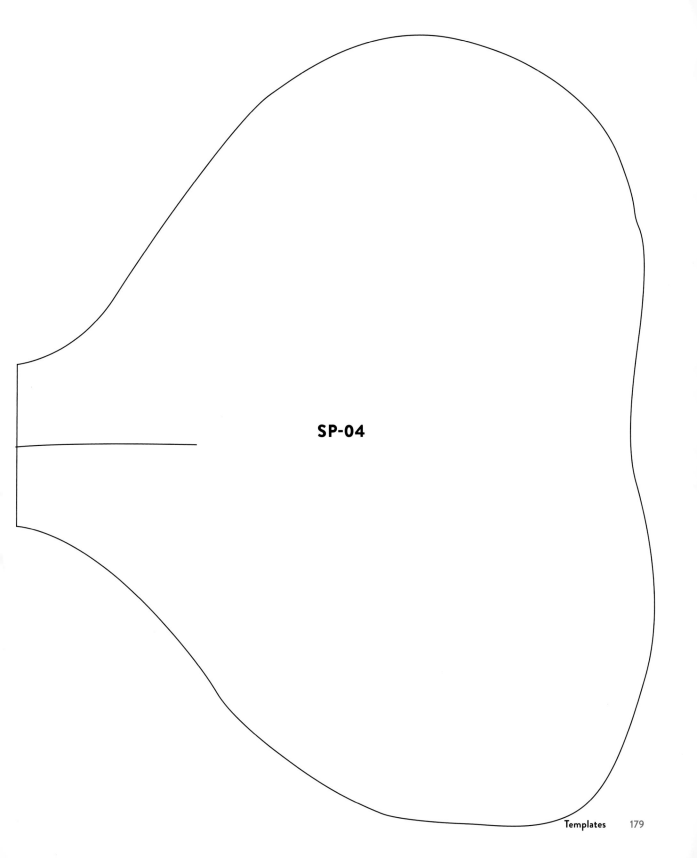

SP-04

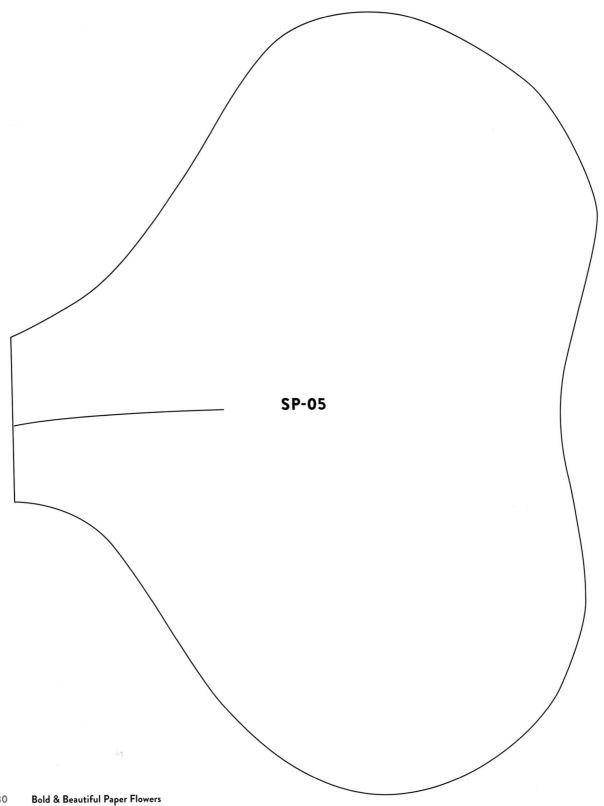

SP-05

SP-06

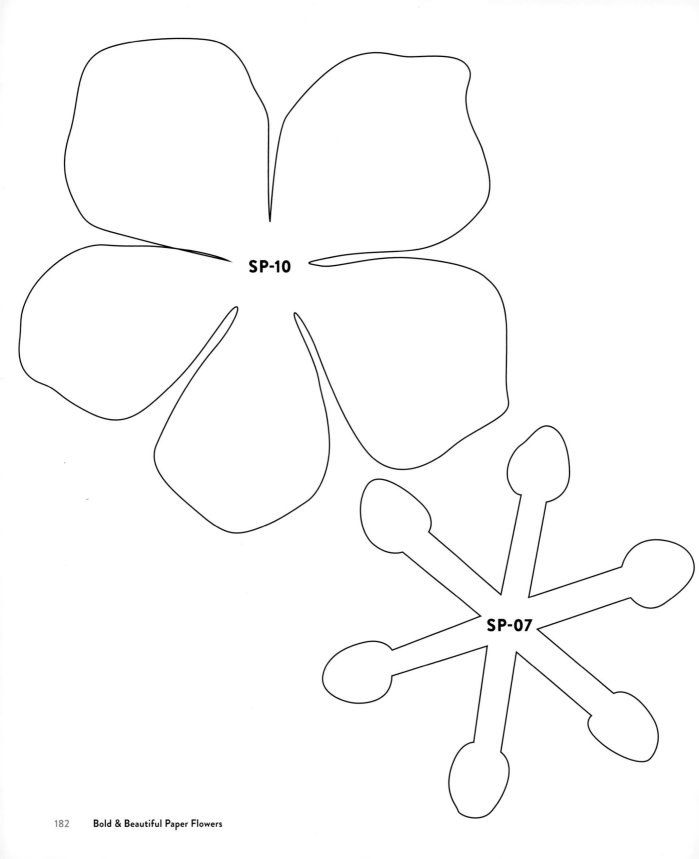

SP-10

SP-07

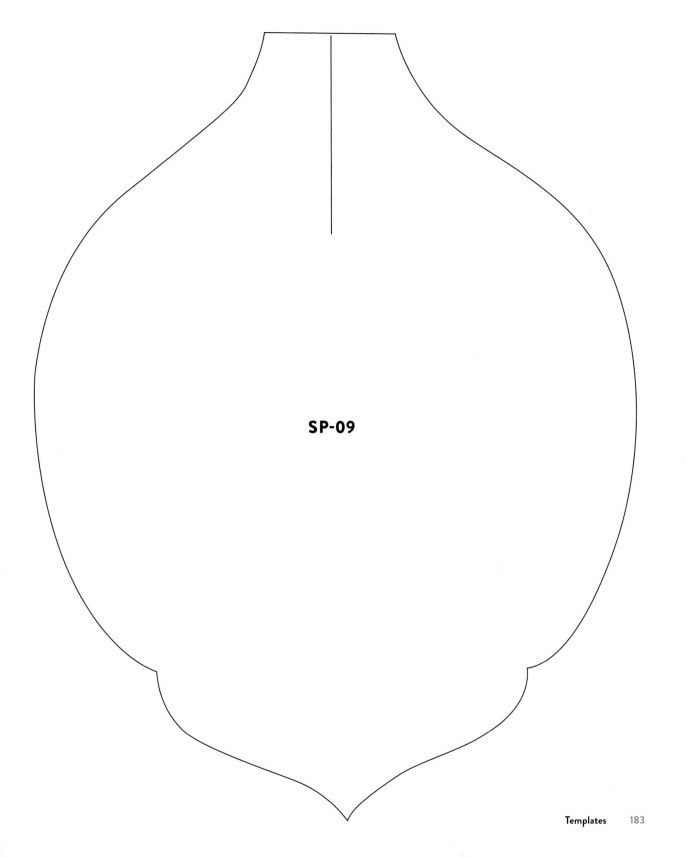

SP-09

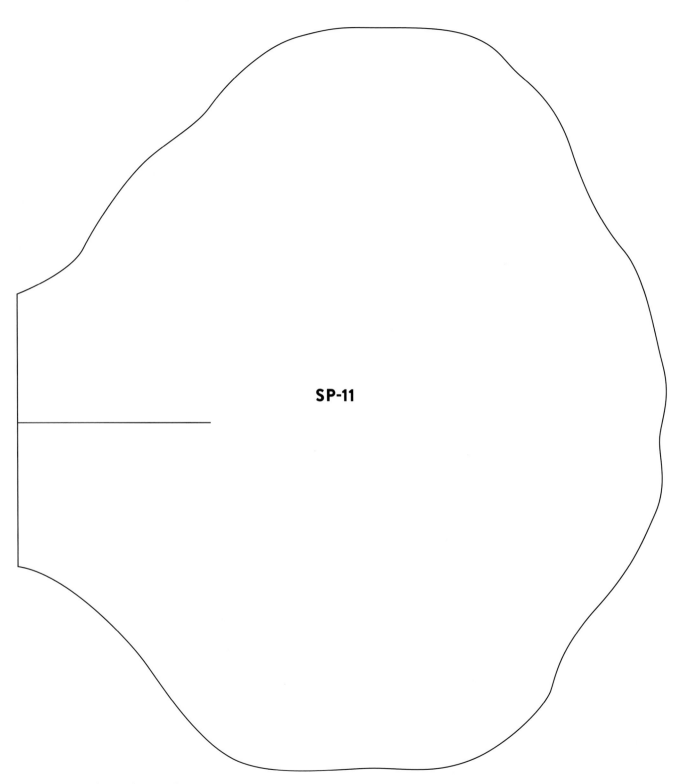

SP-11

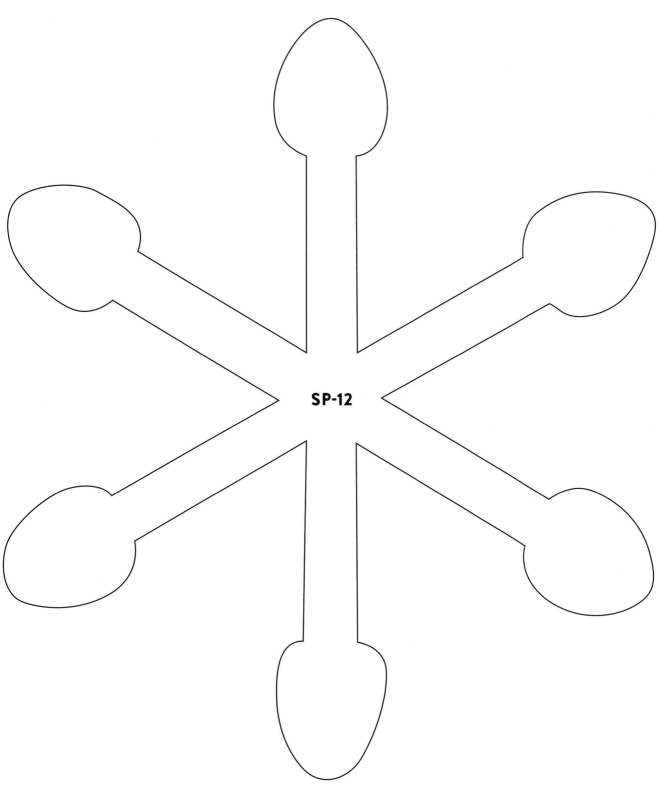

SP-12

CALYXES

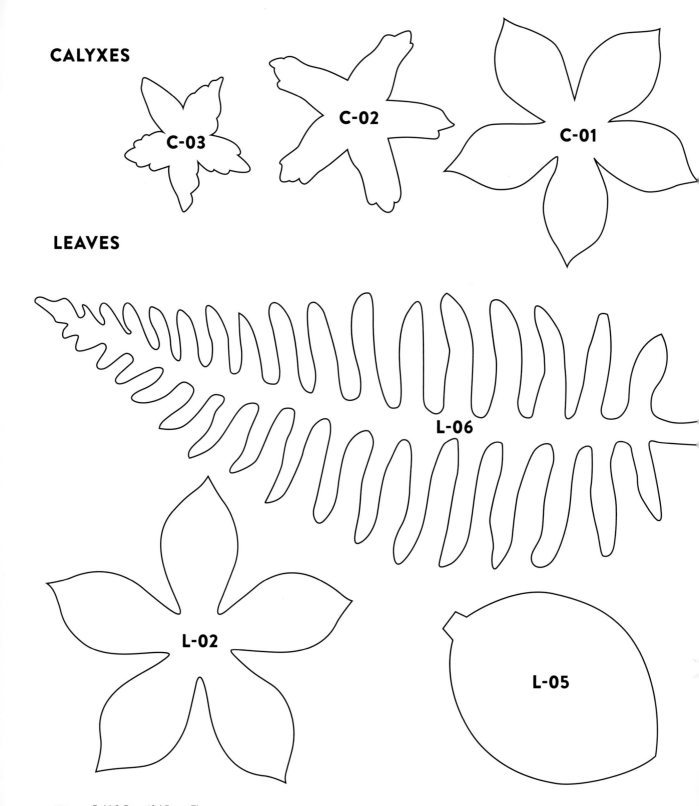

C-03

C-02

C-01

LEAVES

L-06

L-02

L-05

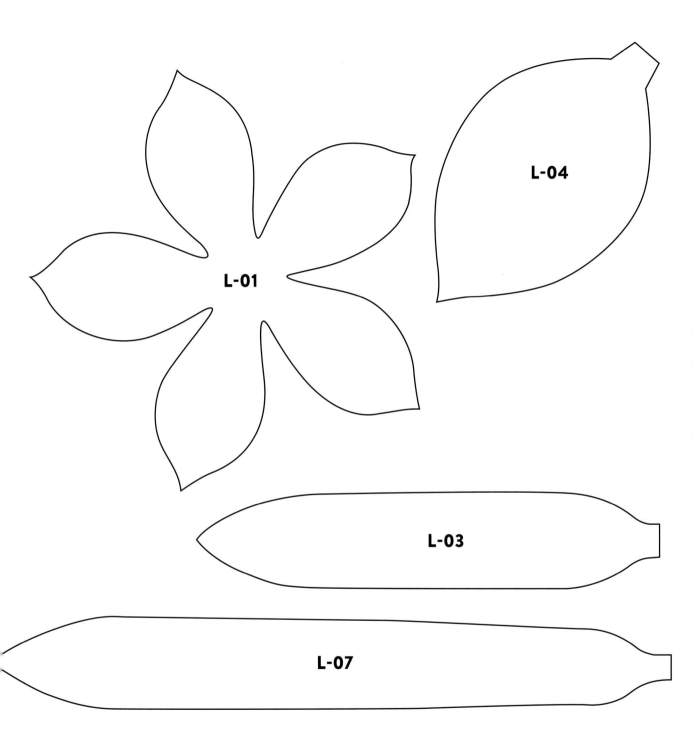

L-04

L-01

L-03

L-07

About the Artist

My passion for floral artistry had very small beginnings, literally. It all started when I needed mini paper flowers to embellish my personal scrapbooking projects. Unable to find what I was looking for, I decided to create tiny paper blooms. When I began listing them on Etsy along with other scrapbooking supplies, I was floored by the high worldwide demand for such items and could barely keep up with the orders!

Eventually, I ventured into the wedding industry—teaching myself how to create all kinds of paper flowers and dreaming up custom arrangements to suit all kinds of celebrations. It was a really steep learning curve, which pushed me to not only stay on top of wedding industry trends, but also to keep developing new skills as the blooms got bigger and designs became more complex.

Through the years, I've had the pleasure of working with thousands of amazing clients!

I especially enjoy when gentlemen send me photos of their wives' wedding bouquets and request a custom paper replica as a thoughtful first-year anniversary gift! An equally touching tribute is when happy clients come back a few years later and ask me to make unique creations for their first baby's nursery!

My love for paper floral design grew with each custom order, and I'm now officially on a mission to embellish people's lives, spaces and fabulous events!

From features in Style Me Pretty and the Perfect Palette to a growing Instagram following of lovelies, it's safe to say that the world has embraced forever blooms too. The marketing initiatives that I've been delighted to collaborate on have surpassed my wildest dreams. Would you believe that my designs have been displayed in Madison Avenue storefronts, at Champagne Perrier-Jouët and Malibu Spiced Rum events, at soirees hosted by "it" girls like Lauren Conrad and Ali Larter, and chosen by Nathalie Dubois for the DPA celebrity gift suite during the 2017 Pre-Golden Globe® Awards Ceremony? Someone please pinch me!

I hope this collection of paper flower projects is just the start of a beautiful creative adventure for you too!

Acknowledgments

I first wish to thank my husband, Renald, whose clever talents and ideas contributed to turning my artistic passion into a flourishing business. I'm especially grateful for his ingenious hacks, which made my workload more manageable.

To Julia and Colin Carslake, who sincerely believed in my gift from the very beginning and so generously helped me bring my dreams to life.

To Kara Ross, whose love and enthusiasm for my floral art paved the way for so many exciting opportunities. I feel blessed to have crossed your path and will be ever thankful that you took the time to share my designs with the world.

To Caroline Langevin, whose branding expertise helped bring Paper & Peony's fabulous image to life and propel it onto the worldwide paper flower scene with confidence: thank you. Her editing of this book also ensured that my readers heard my unique voice—minus the French accent.

To Sarah Monroe, whose professionalism, patience and kind words kept me going during this process. I consider myself very lucky to have been able to work with someone like her on my first book project.

To Christina Re, whose generosity and kind words about my work have inspired me to fly higher and achieve greater.

To everyone who made this book possible:

Mélanie Paulin, owner of Carte Blanche Upcycled Furniture & Accessories

Karen Casey Photography

Caro Photo

Lisa Smith for my awesome hair style and color

Event Decor in a Box

And thank you to countless others who contributed to bringing this book to life.

Finally, a special thank-you to Page Street Publishing for giving me this amazing opportunity to share my art and tell my story.

Index